"'A vulnerable pastor' is often an oxymoroi ~~~~~~ example of her own book. She asks the righ~ ~~~~~~~ and wrestles with the answers—her honesty is honest. Her voice is like a breath of fresh air in an airtight, stuffy room. This isn't a book just for pastors but for all of us who want to be 'real' with ourselves, others and God."

Ruth Graham, author of *In Every Pew Sits a Broken Heart*

"While many pastors are convinced that limitations and messes in ministry are a curse, Mandy Smith shows us that it's in these spaces that God seems to do his most transformative work. Mandy finds the rare and beautiful balance of raw-yet-hopeful and humble-yet-confident vulnerability, while extending grace to the people who seem to need it most: pastors. In today's ministry culture, fraught with the perception of perfection, Mandy offers pastors refreshing permission to be human. But most refreshing of all, she doesn't just write about her message. She does what the most effective authors do—she lives it too."

J.R. Briggs, pastor, author of *Fail* and founder of Kairos Partnerships

"To those with the most impossible of 'jobs'—our pastors—comes a great gift: *The Vulnerable Pastor.* Here, with great care, Mandy Smith manages to reframe what it means to be a pastor and to infuse it with the life of the gospel. I truly tell you that *The Vulnerable Pastor* resonated with the core of my being. It not only made being a pastor possible again, it made being a pastor wonderful."

David Fitch, B. R. Lindner Chair of Evangelical Theology, Northern Seminary, author of *Prodigal Christianity*

"Beautifully written. Irresistibly truthful. *The Vulnerable Pastor* is a profound reversal of nearly everything you know about being a ministry leader. This book exposes the blind spot that the last one hundred years of copying dog-eat-dog, climb-to-the-top leadership models have missed. Vulnerability is the secret to genuine leadership. If the pastoral vocation is to be revived in the decade to come, this is the first aid kit it will need."

Paul Sparks, coauthor of *The New Parish*, cofounding director of Parish Collective

"It's hard to be both painfully honest and faith filled at the same time, but Mandy Smith does it. And she shows us how shepherding souls requires honest faith and hope and love, even when some pain is involved."

Marshall Shelley, editor, *Leadership Journal*

"No kidding: If I could make one new book magically appear on the bedside table of every minister, priest, deacon and elder in North America, *The Vulnerable Pastor* would be it. Mandy Smith's wise and hopeful book is timely, a much-needed antidote to the influence of macho leadership run amok, which has wrecked so many pastors and churches. It is also timeless, an important reminder that God's power is made perfect in weakness. If you are a pastor, please read this book; if you have a pastor, please read it with them."
John Pattison, coauthor of *Slow Church*

"Mandy Smith has packed a lot of freedom for pastors into her book—freedom from unrealistic expectations of others and those they impose on themselves. *The Vulnerable Pastor* creates space and freedom for pastors to embrace honestly their own spiritual journey with God, to engage their struggles, doubts, and dark nights of the soul, and to learn and grow along with those they shepherd. The journey Mandy charts carries enormous potential for enriching their own spiritual journeys as well as deepening their ministries to others. Put simply, she pastors the pastor."
Carolyn Custis James, author of *Half the Church* and *Malestrom*

THE
VULNERABLE
PASTOR

HOW HUMAN LIMITATIONS
EMPOWER OUR MINISTRY

MANDY SMITH

Foreword by DAVID HANSEN

IVP Books

An imprint of InterVarsity Press
Downers Grove, Illinois

InterVarsity Press
P.O. Box 1400, Downers Grove, IL 60515-1426
ivpress.com
email@ivpress.com

InterVarsity Press® is the book-publishing division of InterVarsity Christian Fellowship/USA®, a movement of students and faculty active on campus at hundreds of universities, colleges and schools of nursing in the United States of America, and a member movement of the International Fellowship of Evangelical Students. For information about local and regional activities, visit intervarsity.org.

All Scripture quotations, unless otherwise indicated, are taken from THE HOLY BIBLE, NEW INTERNATIONAL VERSION®, NIV® Copyright © 1973, 1978, 1984, 2011 by Biblica, Inc.™ Used by permission. All rights reserved worldwide.

While any stories in this book are true, some names and identifying information may have been changed to protect the privacy of individuals.

Cover design: Cindy Kiple
Interior design: Beth McGill
Images: Desert landscape: Mark Newman/Getty Images
    Abstract background: ©Vectorig/iStockphoto

ISBN 978-0-8308-4123-3 (print)
ISBN 978-0-8308-9887-9 (digital)

Printed in the United States of America ∞

 As a member of the Green Press Initiative, InterVarsity Press is committed to protecting the environment and to the responsible use of natural resources. To learn more, visit greenpressinitiative.org.

Library of Congress Cataloging-in-Publication Data
Smith, Mandy, 1971-
  The vulnerable pastor : how human limitations empower our ministry / Mandy Smith ; foreword by David Hansen.
    pages cm
  Includes bibliographical references.
  ISBN 978-0-8308-4123-3 (pbk. : alk. paper)
  1. Clergy—Psychology. 2. Clergy—Mental health. 3. Vulnerability (Personality trait) 4. Pastoral theology. I. Title.
BV4398.S57 2015
253'.2--dc23

                                                                  2015027564

| P | 21 | 20 | 19 | 18 | 17 | 16 | 15 | 14 | 13 | 12 | 11 | 10 | 9 | 8 | 7 | 6 | 5 | 4 | 3 | 2 | 1 |
| Y | 33 | 32 | 31 | 30 | 29 | 28 | 27 | 26 | 25 | 24 | 23 | 22 | 21 | 20 | 19 | 18 | 17 | 16 | 15 |

For the good people of University Christian Church.

You have restored my hope in what the church can be.

The joke of it is that often it is the preacher
who as steward of the wildest mystery of them all is
the one who hangs back, prudent, cautious, hopelessly mature
and wise to the last when no less than Saint Paul tells him
to be a fool for Christ's sake, no less than Christ tells him
to be a child for his own and the kingdom's sake.

FREDERICK BUECHNER

Contents

Foreword by David Hansen   9

Introduction: God Is an Odd Leader   11

PART ONE: GETTING OVER OURSELVES
Vulnerability with God

  1 Filled with Emptiness   21

  2 What Makes Us Feel Weak. And What Doesn't   37
     A Confession

  3 Save Me!   47
     Vulnerability and Salvation

  4 Feeling Exposed   60
     How Vulnerable Pastors Handle Emotions

  5 I Need You!   76
     How Vulnerable Pastors Pray

  6 Letting the Bible Read Us   85
     How Vulnerable Pastors Read the Bible

PART TWO: BEING TRUE TO OURSELVES
Vulnerability Behind the Scenes

  7 Learning to Like the Mess   103
     How Vulnerable Pastors Create Culture

  8 Changing the Mold   121
     How Vulnerable Pastors Recognize and Develop Leaders

  9 Taking Our Own Sweet Time   133
     How Vulnerable Pastors Use Their Time and Energy

  10 Thriving for Others   149
     How Vulnerable Pastors Measure Success

PART THREE: PRACTICING IN PUBLIC
Vulnerability with an Audience

    11 Welcome to the Process   165
        How Vulnerable Pastors Teach and Preach

    12 The Right Kind of Desperate   181
        How Vulnerable Pastors Engage with the World

Epilogue: Unfading Treasure in Jars of Clay   193

Discussion Guide   197

Acknowledgments   198

Notes   199

Foreword

by David Hansen

The landscape is littered with pastors who feel inadequate. I count myself as one of them. According to Mandy Smith, we are on the brink of an infusion of power if we embrace our weaknesses and count them as gifts from God. In the process we trust the one God to make up the difference between who we feel we are and what our ministry can become. At least we have the apostle Paul on our side, as he tells the church in Corinth, "Not that we are competent in ourselves to claim anything for ourselves, but our competence comes from God" (2 Corinthians 3:5).

Part of the problem is the tonnage of literature, seminars, lectures and conferences on ministry where leaders call us to pick up their methodologies and follow them. Of course there's nothing wrong with a little rah-rah, common sense and good ideas once in a while, but much of it calls us in the end to raw Promethianism as we allow ourselves to become dominated by a cult of personality and go forth to do the same. We go back home, try things out and they don't work. We feel worse about ourselves than before we started—and, tragically, worse than we really are!

Into this environment Mandy paints a wholly other paradigm. Here is a thoroughgoing exploration of the concept of vulnerability in ministry as strength, as a place to give God the primary place in the equation of ministerial competency. If you're wondering if her vision of ministry grows a church, it just might: her church is growing. I don't mind saying that, not to set up an expectation for your ministry, but to overturn the idea from the start that the picture she paints here—and, by the way, she is a painter, as well as a ridiculously good writer—is a justification for oblivion. This is very real for me, since I pastor an old church of about sixty in a high-crime area of Cincinnati. For us vulnerability isn't an excuse to die. For us vulnerability is a strength as we care for our members and our neighborhood, not knowing what our institutional future may bring.

But it's not just about work in the inner city or the dead spots in rural areas. Her "method" (or shall I say, "unmethod") works in all sorts of ministry environments. The potential is wide; it works with big-church all-togethers who long for a place to be fully human, post-Christian wanderers who can't relate to highfalutin answers, pastors on the brink of burnout and those already over the cliff who are looking for a way to envision ministry again.

It works because Mandy's explication of vulnerability lived out is first and foremost a modus operandi of the Spirit. As such it is demanding. Giving in to the Spirit requires a ruthless release of the self-generating self. If this all sounds like biblical leadership, it should. It is the presupposition of Mary giving her body and soul to the Spirit and Moses leading Israel out of Egypt. As much as these are different tasks and different personalities, they are one strategy: utter reliance on God.

Introduction

God Is an Odd Leader

Our work as pastors is impossible. This is a fact many of us don't learn until we're well into it. In the beginning we see some intelligence, charm or talent in ourselves that makes us think we're up for the challenge of ministry, but inevitably we find it's not enough. We always will if we're doing this work right, for we have been given an impossible task as imperfect beings representing a perfect God. Eventually we find that we have been called to something far beyond us. At some point we will be faced with a sadness too great for our hearts to carry, a question too heavy for our minds, a responsibility that crushes us. When we get there, what will we do? Walk away from a cruel God who would hand us an impossibility? Internalize it as our own failing? Blame everyone around us?

Maybe there's another way. Maybe God gave us an impossible task for a greater purpose.

When we as leaders have an important message or a huge task, we pull out all the stops—lights, music, production. But over and over, when God has some serious business to take care of, he goes small and obscure. Throughout Scripture, when it's time to cast a vision or start a movement, he begins with a child, a pauper or a stranger. He seems to see some kind of renewable resource in human emptiness, a power source in human weakness. Which leads him to make the very odd choice to call us to ministry.

If God's effort to engage with humans were only about communicating ideas, he could do just fine without us. His linguistic skill outstrips anything we bring. But he sees potential in us to express his deepest heart. To tell his story, God often begins with human limitation—a blank canvas where he can begin creating.

Whether or not we talk about it, we're aware of our own limitation. This is especially true when we're faced with the challenges of ministry. We're reminded every day how we're not witty or educated or talented enough. And when we get that sinking feeling of knowing our own limitations, when we're dragged down by the weight of our own emptiness, we want to do whatever we can to fix it. We desperately work harder, hoping that if we're perfect this time it will all be okay. We wear ourselves out, trying to match some preconceived ideal. Or we keep ourselves busy or entertained so we don't have to think about it. And if our own inner voices don't hound us enough, our advertising culture is happy to tell us how to control the pain of our human condition—buy this product, this program, this book, and all our problems will go away.

In the end none of it helps us feel any better about our ability to fulfill our call to ministry. And the more desperate we feel, the more we try to mask how far in over our heads we are, hoping no one will be able to tell.

But this perpetuates the problem. In our efforts to project strength and success, we continue a cycle of unhealthy ideals, setting up unrealistic expectations for others, reproducing something hollow. When we hear only about the strengths and successes of others, it crushes us. And yet we crush others by presenting only our own strengths and successes.

It's time for a new approach. God doesn't need our perfection. He already has his own. He chooses us because we offer something different—humanity. To be what he needs, we can't shy away from our intense experience of weakness. Our stories of human limitation are a kind of confession, and in them we are strangely empowered. When one person is willing to step into vulnerability, it disrupts forever the cycle that traps us, giving us permission to share our fears, creating a space for others to be human and for God to be God.

One of the most encouraging moments in my ministry was when Hayden, a seminary student who attends my church, said, "When I see how you do ministry, for the first time I see that I could do ministry." The hope I saw in his eyes is what I want to share with others who may not feel they can do it. Because, ironically, the way I do ministry has grown out of a deep sense of my inability to do it. Hayden was not looking at my great skill, only at the way I have learned to laugh at my inadequacy and keep on working. We admit weakness not only to be free from the shame of our limitations but also to turn to a true source of power.

> What discipline is required for the future leader to overcome the temptation of individual heroism? I would like to propose the discipline of confession.
> **Henri J. M. Nouwen**[1]

Don't get me wrong. I'm not naturally comfortable talking about vulnerability. I'm painfully aware that my writing is filled with first-person pronouns. I'd much rather talk about impersonal ideas. But confessions begin with "I."

It began with confession to my congregation, with my need to break out of the silent shame of my limitations, trusting Bonhoeffer's wisdom that when we confess to a fellow believer, we are no longer alone but we experience the presence of God in that person.[2]

And what do I confess? Not sin in the way we usually understand it. And yet it is a "falling short of the glory," an unhealthy appetite of a different kind. I confess that I am vulnerable. Not simply that I *feel* vulnerable, but that I am inherently susceptible to weakness, inadequacy. And that in response I try to compensate, to be invincible, to be God. If it was their efforts to be like God that had Adam and Eve expelled from the garden, this is serious confession.

In confessing for my own sake, I've watched how it's given grace to others, how it's breaking a culture of performance, perfectionism and shame. And so although it's uncomfortable, I'm happy to extend that confession to a broader community in the form of a book, albeit a book with a lot of the word "I."

Another reason I'm uncomfortable talking about vulnerability is because the discussion naturally turns to issues of gender. In my conversations with women and minorities, I've seen the unique challenges we face. I don't like to talk like a victim, but there are certainly many times when, directly and indirectly, I have been told my voice is less valid than others'—so finding it has taken more grace and courage than you might think. We could say that the history of marginalization reflects the failure of those in power, yet it doesn't stop the marginalized from feeling like failures. It's hard for anyone to admit weakness. It's even harder for the marginalized as they work to be taken seriously in a world not their own.

While the marginalized are figuring that out, those of us in leadership feel the added pressure of an audience. While I don't have a chip on my shoulder, as the only female lead pastor in my fellowship of some six thousand churches, I feel the pressure to be perfect.[3] Even as I ask myself, *Can I do this?* I know there are many watching me who are also asking, *Can she do this?* They're assessing my attitude, the success of my church, the power of my preaching—and even if it's mostly with good intentions or curiosity, it puts pressure on me to be strong. So it's even harder to admit how very much I'm weak.

I don't want this to be "A Female Pastor's Guide to Ministry," but I am a female pastor. I realize the cliché—a woman writing a book about weakness and vulnerability. But I'm not naturally good at it. Everything in my education and culture has taught me to put on a good front, to work extra hard behind the scenes so that my performance is faultless. When you're the first woman *anything* you have to be better at it to be taken seriously. Taking myself seriously worked for a while. But before long it was ludicrous. My only choice was to throw up my hands and laugh.

I can laugh because confessing inadequacy has taught me this: If feeling our own weakness makes us rely on God, and if the best ministry grows from reliance on him, then our weakness is a ministry resource. And we have an unlimited supply of this resource. With this approach, learning to embrace weakness has made me feel strangely invincible! The things that used to bring shame and fear now force me to tell those I lead, "Well, we're just going to have to trust God because I'm so inadequate it's funny!"

I'll tell the story as it unfolded for me: first in a deeply personal place, then with my church leaders, then with the congregation, then with the broader world. Allowing the questions to begin in my own life meant I had to trust that I was not the only one asking them. Whether we're talking about an individual's experience or the experience of the billions who inhabit this earth, we're talking about vulnerable human experience.

This question of what it means to be human is one of the most important questions we can ask. And important questions should be handled in important ways, which often means in detached, formal ways. I started there when I first asked this question, but my nice, detached ideas kept burrowing themselves back into their birthplace—my own life. Eventually I had to stop fighting and let them stay there, not because it's comfortable asking important questions in a very personal way but because when the questions are about humanity, the investigation of them must be a human one. If we believe the same truth expresses itself in Scripture, the world and our lives, we can make our lives a study of how the truth of our human vulnerability and our need for God remain singular and yet reveal many facets.

> God is one. But God also reveals himself in various ways that at first don't always seem to fit together.... It is always the same God, but the "person" or the "face" or "voice" by which we receive the revelation varies. But here's the thing: every part of the revelation, every aspect, every form is personal—God is relational at the core—and so whatever is said, whatever is revealed, whatever is received is also personal and relational. There is nothing impersonal, nothing merely functional, everything from beginning to end and in between is personal. God is inherently and inclusively personal.
>
> **Eugene Peterson**[4]

This has been my approach as I have worked to figure out how God in Scripture, God in my life and God in the world can be One. I write to share how I wrestled with these questions as I adjusted to long-term life in the United States as a transplant from Australia and as I transitioned, within just two years, from associate to co-lead pastor to lead pastor. I share the lessons I learned as I figured out what it meant to lead University Christian Church (UCC), a campus and neighborhood congregation and fair-trade café in uptown Cincinnati. But I trust that the result is more than memoir. As Esther Lightcap Meek puts it, "Insight isn't informational; it is transformational."[5]

To keep this from remaining only my story, there are invitations throughout for you to wrestle yourself, opportunities to reflect on how the story connects with God's movement in your story. And so while this book is not theology or exegesis in the usual sense, I hope that it is thoroughly theological and exegetical. I don't tell my story because I think it's so unusual but because our stories share a common human theme. Step with me into this trust that things that seem deeply personal have global ramifications and things that seem global have deeply personal ramifications.

We'll begin with personal questions: When we sense we're not all we should be to fulfill our calling, will it be our undoing? Or will it hold some new potential? If God called humans to lead his church, is it okay for us to be human? How is our culture intolerant of weakness and what weakness fixes does it offer?

We'll confess how we deny our intrinsic vulnerabilities, how instead of approaching God from need we try to earn our own salvation (and what that means for our evangelistic efforts). We'll confess our efforts to dominate emotion, to manipulate God through prayer, to tame Scripture, to control church culture, to force leaders into our mold. We'll confess how we desire to be superhumanly productive and successful, to determine the development of others. We'll confront our overcompensation for the powerlessness we feel when we can't fix everything, can't understand everything, can't hold back the post-Christian tide.

And these confessions will free us to step into healthier habits: following, praying, feeling, creating, communicating and engaging in new ways, unafraid of vulnerability. We will discover a leadership that's comfortable with following.

This new approach reveals untapped leadership potential. It renews energy from burnout. It uncovers opportunities for God to work not only in spite of, but because of our weakness. It teaches us how he can work in and through the people he has made us to be right now. It helps us name our fears and limitations for the sake of acknowledging our need for him, freeing us from the need to be enough. That freedom will change how we see this moment in the history of the church. As the world changes and Christianity falls from power, we will see how God can reveal his power even through our lack of political sway. In the end, what better Christian leadership can there be than the kind that models a deep trust in him? He chooses us in all our inadequacy so that when it's all said and done, there's no question whose power was at work.

PART ONE

GETTING OVER OURSELVES

Vulnerability with God

1

Filled with Emptiness

The week I stepped into my new role as co-lead pastor I attended a major convention for Christian leaders. For four years I had served as associate pastor alongside my good friend and lead pastor Troy Jackson, and then his growing passion for justice work led us to reduce his workload at UCC to allow him to pursue those opportunities. As we were entering this new partnership, I attended the conference with an open heart, hoping it would equip me for what was ahead. It certainly did, but not in the way I expected.

The more workshops I attended and bookstands I perused, the more strange I felt. Something didn't feel right. I sat in the sessions and earnestly took notes, waiting for something to connect, but the harder I tried, the more I felt myself sinking. After a day of this discomfort, I found myself at dinner with some of the key speakers. I was surprised to hear myself ask them, "Do you ever feel like you're making it up as you go along?"

I know they responded to me, but I have no recollection of what they said because none of it gave me what I was really asking for—a glimpse behind the scenes into their human hearts. I'm sure they left wondering, "Who was that awkward person with her odd questions?"

I went to bed that night feeling defeated, but in the morning I psyched myself up for another day.

It was more of the same: programs to plug in that would fix my problems. Systems to integrate that would manage my congregants. Books to buy that would prop up my insecurities. Everything was intended for good, but it was not for me. The programs and measurements of success did not represent me. The assumptions didn't include me (statements like "All leaders will be motivated by . . . " and "Your church doesn't want a leader like this; they want a man who . . ."). As far as I could tell, no one in this huge gathering of church leaders looked or sounded or thought like me. I hadn't gone with a chip on my shoulder, expecting to be marginalized. In fact, I had expected to be welcomed and included. But by midday, the sinking feeling returned with greater intensity and I faked a coughing fit to mask my teary departure. Feeling shame at my emotional state, I headed for my hotel room, where I told God, *This job isn't for me. I have nothing to give. You've made a mistake.*

The realization was so disturbing to me—at forty years of age, after years of prayer and preparation for this role—that for the next twenty-four hours I couldn't leave my little hotel room. It's a blur to me now but I remember bouts of tears, dry retching, restless sleep and the kind of prayer that scrapes your insides on its way out. The place inside of me where I go to draw on strength or faith or feeling was a wasteland. If a fire could scorch a desert and leave it drier and deader than it already had been, that was the state of my soul. I longed for God to comfort me with words like, "You're stronger than you think" and "You've got this—look at all the gifts I've given you!" But instead, in my despair, God's voice was assuring but vague.

A broken and contrite spirit I will not despise.

In your weakness I am strong.

Deep truths that felt flat compared to the empty expanse in my soul.

Yeah, yeah, God, I know. Keep trusting in your strength . . . still . . . again.

Although I awoke the next day with eyes swollen closed from crying and my stomach still churning, I knew I had to return to the world. I grabbed something for my headache and invented an explanation for my red eyes. I got through the conference and returned to my home and work, still raw from the experience. We often joke that going to a conference is like drinking from a fire hose. What do you do when it's more like gulping for air as the torrents threaten to drown you?

A SHAKY BEGINNING

And so I began this new phase of leadership not with assurances of my own ability but with a mental map of every hollow of the cavernous emptiness within me. And yet a sense of God's strength was enough for me to falteringly step into the work before me. As I did, God helped me get over the rawness of the emptiness and, in the process, get over myself.

When I have no words for my feelings I make a collage. Flipping through magazines and cutting out what resonates (without having to explain why) is like taking a glossy Rorschach test. After hacking up several magazines I had two piles of clippings. In one I gathered:

- I'm embarrassed
- Mistake
- Creative
- Imperfect
- Experimental
- Trust
- Endurance

- Music
- Open
- Jazz
- Free
- Bare it
- Imagination
- A little picture of a naked man riding a bike

The second pile of clippings included:

- Fear
- Win
- Live life on center stage
- Be fabulous
- Control
- Achieve

- Safety (twice)
- Paralysis
- Image
- Feeling like you've sold your soul
- Several images of shiny armor
- A woman in a killer pair of heels

I knew there was a choice to make between a life of safety, control and adulation (which felt good but also seemed like a compromise of something valuable) and the risky, experimental life of freedom and heart (which seemed like the right choice but also scared me to death). The scary choice seemed to lead toward God, and yet how could God expect it of me? One thing I knew for sure: I had never been more aware that I was completely limited. I had never felt so filled to the brim with emptiness. This was not the way I expected leadership to feel!

My choices warred in me. (Why couldn't I just keep the best of both? Could I be on an adventure but still be in total control?) So I played out this war with my paints. It felt right to finger paint first with yellow—thick and lumpy—on a huge old door. Finger painting feels like childhood, like freedom under your fingernails. But when the paint was dry and knobbly, two large black

> When the safety net has split, when the resources are gone, when the way ahead is not clear, the sudden exposure can be both frightening and revealing. We spend so much of our time protecting ourselves from this exposure that a weird kind of relief can result when we fail. To lie flat on the ground with the breath knocked out of you is to find a solid resting place. This is as low as you can go. You told yourself you would die if it ever came to this, but here you are. You cannot help yourself and yet you live.
> **Barbara Brown Taylor**[1]

crayon squares wanted to impose themselves on the fun. Strong and perfect (if you're a *Star Trek* fan, think the Borg), they wanted to corral the mess. And yet the texture of the yellow kept the black from overcoming and bits of yellow broke through everywhere. After so many hard, dark lines, it was time for some playfulness again and this time green paint squirted itself with abandon across the board, pleasing me with the way it formed tendrils. But the darkness couldn't abide such joy so, in the form of black shoe polish, it swirled and billowed, threatening to cloud out the life and color. In places it grayed the brightness, but one little green tendril defiantly held back the cloud.

As I painted, my heart cheered on the color and playfulness, humming all along ("I will sing, sing a new song. How long to sing this song?"), hoping it would win but fearing it wouldn't. The result of my work could have been a scene from Revelation, but instead of a dragon there were black squares and gray clouds, and the woman had become yellow swirls and green life. I know who overcomes in the end. Without even knowing how to step away from the comfort of black squares, that day I chose to step into the freedom—and vulnerability—of green life.

> Security is mostly a superstition. It does not exist in nature, nor do the children of men as a whole experience it. . . . Avoiding danger is no safer in the long run than outright exposure. Life is either daring adventure, or nothing.
> **Helen Keller**[2]

DARING ADVENTURE OR NOTHING

At this time a friend shared with me the now-famous TED talks on vulnerability by Brené Brown, who might as well have turned to the camera and addressed me personally as she stated, "Vulnerability is not weakness. Vulnerability is pure courage," and "Vulnerability is the birthplace of joy, creativity, belonging and love."[3]

How does one lead with vulnerability? I'd never seen it done so I had no choice but to jump in. Learning on the job is hard at the best of times. I'd been dropped into the deep end at work before, trying to run a sandwich shop while the lunch line snaked out the door. No one had showed me how to make ten sandwiches at a time while also working the register. But now I was learning on the job before an audience of 160. The stakes were much higher than messing up a few sandwiches.

Now I was stepping into an iconic role—The Pastor—which was not unlike how it had felt to become The Mother. I was living a stereotype: The Pastor is always kind, patient and wise but also strong, capable and decisive. The Pastor can never say, "Can I have a week to make that decision?" or "Can I avoid difficult people when trying to write sermons?" And The Pastor doesn't express unfiltered feelings—exasperation or annoyance—and certainly never has a full-on sobbing meltdown. The Pastor must reflect nothing less than God himself at all times.

PRACTICING IN PUBLIC

It seems I had more to learn about improvisation. I had been so proud years before when I taught myself to play music by heart. Controlling every note had made my performance consistently good, but improvising meant it could be great at the risk of being terrible. Back then I was in a band with six other musicians, so my terrible was covered. Now I was becoming a soloist of sorts and my mistakes were glaringly obvious. Couldn't I just step aside for six months? A year? To figure out in private how to do this and come back when I was ready? I never asked to practice in public.

I journaled. "Is it my role to fail well? To live an example of brokenness in a public sphere so that others have permission to fail? To give myself grace and say, 'I'm sorry,' and trust grace will be given?"

The following pages remained blank.

Brennan Manning came to my side through his memoir, *All Is Grace*, which opens with a Leonard Cohen poem:

Ring the bells that still can ring.
Forget your perfect offering.
There is a crack in everything.
That's how the light gets in.[4]

I copied it onto a chalkboard by my back door and it's still there, years later.

In the margins of Manning's book, I scribbled, "Reading this story of a man whose alcoholism drove him to God and gave him a deep understanding of, and ministry of, grace makes me wonder if God doesn't use us in spite of our brokenness but because of it."

Here was the beginning of resurrection. A little seed had been planted in me and something living was beginning to shoot from it. Another "friend," Henri Nouwen, came to cultivate it with these words: "The Christian leader of the future is called . . . to stand in this world with nothing to offer but his or her own vulnerable self."[5]

But who was this self I was to offer? I felt like an insecure teenager all over again as I dug inside to work out what God saw in me—and came up with very little. Which is when a trusted mentor cautioned, "Maybe there are messages you're believing that aren't from God."

So I set to making a list of the false messages I believed. Here's what I wrote:

- I need to perfectly reflect God's character at all times, never get angry, never upset anyone, never make mistakes.

- I need to represent women pastors well, especially with how I express my feelings and how I look. I should never be girly or frumpy or remind anyone of the baggage they have with their mothers.

- I need to present only fully developed intellectual ideas. My playfulness, stories, creativity and emotion are childish and less significant than ideas and arguments.

[handwritten margin notes: ICH MUSS STARK SEIN; LEUTE URTEILEN ÜBER MICH; IN THE END OF THE DAY I'M ALONE; UND ALLE GELBEN]

- I need to live up to others' standards.

- I can't have needs.

- I need to make everyone happy.

- My voice is smaller and less valuable than others'.

Reflect

What are the false messages you believe? Invite a trusted friend to help you name them.

Santa Claus God and Slave Driver God

It was surprising how quickly I could put into words this unspoken self-talk that daily circled my head. And it was surprising how, once out of me, these lies became repulsive. I wanted to step away from them but didn't know what to step toward. I longed to discover what it could look like to lead from the heart, to have joy in my role, to work without the burden of performance and duty.

These questions were pressing because all the while I was taking on more and more responsibility. While I was questioning what it meant to fill this co-lead pastor role (and the conference I'd turned to for encouragement had left me even less confident), I never considered stepping down. Not out of courage but out of obligation. I was a workhorse, ready to take the load. My co-lead, Troy, was being called into new ministry opportunities, things I'd encouraged him to pursue, and I didn't want to let him down. When all the leadership transition dust settled it suddenly dawned on me that I'd taken on much more responsibility than I'd anticipated. I was resentful.

I'm trying to raise a family and support my husband in his ministry. Being an associate pastor has been stressful enough! God, why would you lay more on my shoulders?

I stepped into the well-worn slave track. I knew the routine: bear the load so that others can be blessed by God. Don't complain, do your duty, override your needs and desires. I still hadn't discovered how to lead from the heart or have joy in my role. A good friend cautioned me, "If you run in your own strength, at best you will have earthly success." It sounded wise—but how to run in God's strength?

When others heard my description of my slave driver God, they reminded me, "No, you're a child of the king. Whatever you ask, you will receive." And so I flipped from slave driver God to Santa Claus God. From feeling the weight of his demands I shifted to making demands, listing all the ways I'd worked out that God should behave so I would feel loved.

He didn't do any of it. And I don't blame him.

I'm sure God grew tired of swapping his whip and scowl for a sack of toys and a jolly grin, many times within one day. And I grew tired of swinging from overburdened victim to pouty, demanding child. As much as I knew neither caricature reflected reality, I had no idea what was true. In desperation I prayed, "God, these roles I'm casting us in feel right because I've seen them played out in human relationships. But their familiarity doesn't make them true. Could you remind me of an experience that's more like the truth?"

And the fastest answer to prayer I've ever received came in the form of a memory.

I was nine and watching TV in those glorious hours between school and dinner, when my dad called out that he was fixing the car and needed help bleeding the brakes. A little part of me was disappointed to step away from my favorite show. But a different part of me was honored to be asked, especially since it involved sitting in the driver's seat. I was sure the neighbors would be impressed. I knew my part: pull the seat forward so I could reach the brake and just wait for my dad's directions.

"Press it halfway down!"

"That's right. Now all the way down!"

"Let it up now."

"Good job!"

I knew I was part of something significant, even though my part was small, and it was an honor that my dad had asked for my help.

This was a totally new way to understand my relationship with God. He is not a demanding slave driver, sitting in the shade while I do his bidding, assessing my performance from afar. Neither is he a sentimental old fool, set on keeping me in perpetual childhood. He is an active Father, at work in the world, honoring me by inviting me to walk with him into the adventure. How could I say no? How could I apologize for the lies I'd believed? For the burden I'd felt in his invitation? I'd missed the invitation because I'd expected it to feel cozy, but there it was, hiding in the challenge. The challenge became an invitation to be where God was.[6]

THE SILENT MOTIVATOR

Now came the biggest challenge of all: trusting that it really could be true, that a God who loved me was calling me to receive his love in deeper ways than I ever had. Maybe it was all just a fairy story made up by weak people to soothe themselves. How could I prove to anyone that God loved me? How could I prove it to myself? When I looked at people who'd had the courage to step into his love, I saw wholeness and freedom. When I remembered others who weren't willing to risk believing that they were loved, their bitterness and fear felt like the weight of what I wanted to leave behind. And so I experienced a moment of salvation. I wanted freedom and wholeness. And although I didn't understand it, I stepped toward it. I had been a believer for thirty years, and yet it was like coming to faith for the first time. I chose to trust his love.

Perfect love casts out fear. And although I'd never put them into words, just as quickly as I had been able to write out the lies I believed,

I was able to list my fears:

- I will make bad decisions.
- I will upset someone.
- It won't work out.
- Money and people won't come.
- It will be messy.
- I will be embarrassed.
- I will mishear God.
- I will forget or overlook something important.

If you've ever read the Harry Potter books, you may remember the mandrake root, a strange, misshapen thing that screams a deathly scream when unearthed. It seemed to me that my fears were just as uncomfortable seeing the light of day. As children we can name our fears—spiders, thunder, darkness. Adult fears are more subtle and Satan loves for them to go unnamed. Because then he can use them as silent motivators, steering us down whatever course avoids as many fears as possible, keeping us cautious and reactionary.

Reflect

What are you motivated to avoid? What fears underlie these motivations?

[handwritten margin notes: BEING LONELY / LEFT BEHIND / TO FAIL / TO BE HURT]

It was a grace that God helped me name my fears, because a new challenge was on the horizon. After just one year of sharing the co-lead role, Troy and I saw something new begin to unfold. I saw his love for his justice work and he saw my potential for church leadership. As we encouraged each other, we saw that our fates were intertwined. And so after

eighteen years as lead pastor, Troy stepped fully into his new call, leaving
me to step fully into mine as lead pastor of UCC. And although my sense
of inadequacy was just as strong as it had been in my previous transition,
I must have learned something, because I remember telling myself the
vague, slightly flaky and yet incredibly satisfying statement, "I am enough
to continue the process of becoming more (but still never enough)."

One night during this period I had a dream. It was a simple scene of
a church service in our sanctuary. While the congregation prayed I knelt
with them in the front row. Raising my eyes a moment, I was alarmed
to see a cloud of dust filling the air above us, threatening to overshadow
the service, to blind and smother us. But my fear gave way to peace.
From my position kneeling on the floor, I blew a tiny puff of breath, not
enough to budge a dandelion seed. In an instant the overwhelming
cloud dispersed to nothing. *Pfft!* To this day, when I feel overwhelmed
by the clouds gathering (and I often do), I sometimes blow this little
puff of breath as my prayer that I will do what small thing I can and
trust God to make it what it needs to be. By the time the lead pastor
role began, I knew that it could happen only in God's strength.

Until one moment almost undid it all.

It was one of my first days to preach as lead pastor and I was still
learning the new weight of this work. Before the service, as I welcomed people by the door, I saw a couple looking for seats. When
I recognized them, my heart sank. They were people I loved and
admired and they had a deep history with this congregation. But
they didn't believe women should preach. My first thought was, *I'll
just be so darn good at this preaching thing that they'll have to reconsider
their ideas about women.* But when I turned inward to find that great
skill to draw from, I found only the scorched wasteland I'd visited
in the hotel room.

If I could be really good at this, people might see that I should do
it. But what about when I wasn't really good at it? Did that mean I

shouldn't do it? Standing by the back door, I looked down the aisle to the place where I was soon to stand and preach. God asked me, *Do you believe I put you here?*

All my performance anxiety fell away as I found myself quietly saying (and believing), *Yes.*

By the time I stood to preach, I was listening to his heart for his people and praying that what I said would connect them to him, even those people who didn't think I should be speaking on his behalf.

This experience rewired my brain. In the past anxiety had motivated me to work harder, live up to some imagined ideal, hope I'd make a good impression. Oh, and if everything else failed, to pray and ask for help. But by calling my attention away from my fears and toward his call, God broke me out of that rut. I could have freedom because I was no longer working in my own strength or from my own authority.

Reflect

Where do you find your authority?

Stepping Away from Safe Little Cities

This new way of trusting made me ready to revisit my hotel room experience. That room felt like a tomb in my memory, so I took the Lord of all tombs there to show me how resurrection could begin.

On Good Friday I found an old board in the garage and starting painting. I filled the left side of the board with a depiction of my former life, some combination of the tower of Babel and hell as depicted by C. S. Lewis in *The Great Divorce*—human efforts at strength and control. The image became a flat little gray city, very orderly but lifeless. Then I set about lighting a fire in the center of the board, and with some creative use of kindling, the wood smoldered slowly. When the flame was extinguished, I was satisfied to see my dark dryness of soul reflected back at me from the blackened board. It was scorched and barren, like that little gray city had gone through a great fire from which no life could ever grow.

Then I squirted red and orange and green paint, spreading it with my fingers, letting it fly straight from the bottle without regard for where it would fall. Somehow it was at the same time both a wild plant bursting with blossoms and a fire alive with light. The city was no more, but in its place raged a burning bush, not safe but good. When I saw the light and life that grew from that dark, dry place and knew it expressed what was happening in me, I did not miss that safe little city one bit.

Now, years after that conference and my hotel room desert experience, I've looked lies and fears square in the eye. While they still rear their ugly heads, now that I've named them, I recognize them for what they are and the power they have over me is diminished. This frees me to step into the truth that God calls all his people into, limited as we are—to follow and serve him. We can see our limitations and cringe in shame or we can choose to see the potential in them. We can see the opportunity to rely even more on God and, in that reliance, to find unlimited resources for our work.

> We often hear that humanness involves only two dimensions: ourselves and our situation. Humanness is successfully coping with our situation. But the Void—the deep realization that we might not exist, that we need something, someone, beyond ourselves—is actually an important third dimension of our humanness. … If we deny the threat, or resign ourselves to it, we aren't doing the healing thing with the Void. The healing thing is to admit our need truthfully and cry out for deliverance. This is what happens when we come to the end of ourselves and start to look in hope beyond ourselves for help. We open ourselves to what we cannot manufacture and cannot presume to deserve. We open ourselves to what can only come graciously: the possibility of new being.
>
> **Esther Lightcap Meek**[7]

THE WAY OF WEAKNESS

Often when we feel our weakness, it comes like an assault, raining blows that taunt, *You're not enough*. There are three common ways we respond to an assault: flee in fear, get knocked down or brace ourselves and come out fighting. If we choose to flee, our culture offers substances that numb and lights that dazzle to distract us from our emptiness. If we let weakness knock us down, our culture calls us losers, failures, and it looks away in disgust. If we choose to engage the assault, our world offers weapons for the fight—products to buy, books to read, goals to accomplish, technology to utilize—to fortify our soft arms. Regardless of the response we choose, the more we numb, the more we give in, the harder we fight it, the more we know we're desperately not enough.

But there's a fourth way to respond to an assault, one that feels like judo. Instead of avoiding, absorbing or defending against the blows that come our way, we can roll with them. We'll still feel an initial impact, but if we're responsive we can take the force directed against us and redirect it. So anything that is intended for evil, God can use for good. Anything.

Reflect

How do you feel you don't measure up? What is it about you that you fear disqualifies you from ministry?

Read 2 Corinthians 12:5-10. What weaknesses, insults, hardships, persecutions, difficulties could you delight in? How are they opportunities to show God's strength?[8]

When we see how God is able to show his power in our weakness, not in spite of our weakness but because of it, we are no longer ashamed or afraid. When we see the expansive task at hand and instead of fullness in ourselves find only a gaping void in our own ability, we have no choice but to call on the fullness of God. When we see the ridiculous disparity between our skill and the great need, there's nothing for it but to laugh, throw up our hands and declare, "I'm so unfit it's funny! The need is so huge only God can fill it. We have no choice but to trust him!" Then we can not only resign ourselves to weakness, we can boast in it.

This may feel like navel-gazing (and it may have to begin there), but it has the potential to transform our lives and ministries. Christian leaders can be human again; the church can show a human face to the world again. Beyond answering my personal questions and identity issues, this approach has grown into the integrated philosophy of ministry that I share in the pages ahead, one that has changed every aspect of my work. Not only has it made ministry more sustainable and enjoyable for me, it is showing fruit in the life of my staff and congregation as together we watch what God can do in and through us, because of us and in spite of us. How would our work look if we really embraced and boasted in our limitations? What could it mean to be experts in weakness?[9]

2

What Makes Us Feel Weak.
And What Doesn't

A Confession

When we're children, we're unashamed to say, "I don't know" or "I need help." But somewhere in our socialization, we learn that such things are not to be voiced. By the time we reach adulthood, we've developed an array of tricks to mask our ignorance and weakness; we've mastered our facial expressions so no one can tell when we feel in over our heads. And we assume we're the only ones pretending.

In addition to experiencing social pressure that makes weakness shameful, we have the comfort and convenience of First-World wealth, which can shield us from our human limitations for years. And then when we lose our job or can't heal our child or don't understand our spouse, we think God has abandoned us. The anomaly is the years of ease and confidence, not our human limitation. The anomaly is that we are a small population in the history of the world that has to be coached on how to see our own vulnerability. If we are to pastor vulnerable humans *as* vulnerable humans, we have to unlearn the habits of putting on a strong front.

Since technology is a big part of our blindness to our need, let's consider the role it plays. Christian philosopher Albert Borgmann offers insight here by comparing a finely crafted musical instrument

to a stereo. To master the playing of an instrument, we must engage
with it over time. It takes physical skill, creative sensitivity and perse-
verance. And when we watch a musician perform on an instrument, it
inspires our hearts and captures the attention of both our eyes and
ears. On the other hand, a stereo can at the touch of a button provide
more consistent quality and a broader range of music. With very little
skill we can control the selection of music, the volume, when it starts,
when it stops. As Borgmann says, "We respect a musician; we own a
stereo." He goes on to reveal how we have many choices in life like
this. We don't have to look far to see that "devices and consumption
have replaced things and practices." The age-old art of cooking has
become microwaving packaged food. The practice of storytelling has
been replaced by watching TV. Instead of navigating the terrain, we
zip along smooth highways. Instead of engaging with seasons and
bugs, we have technologies for growing more food faster.[1]

The technology is always faster, easier and (seemingly) simpler than
the traditional option. It gives us more control. But it often has an
invisible or delayed cost. When doing yard work, I can trim my hedge
in twenty minutes with a pair of hedge shears or I can do it in five
minutes with an electric hedge trimmer. There would seem to be no
contest! But with the hedge shears I enjoy the satisfying "thwack!"
with each cut and tone my arms at the same time. The electric trimmer
pollutes the air with noise and uses up nonrenewable resources. While
hand trimming takes more time, it engages me with nature, con-
necting me to my Eden ancestors, sensibly subduing without domi-
nating. Electric trimming feels like I've completed a task; hand
trimming feels like good work. I may reflect or invent during the
rhythmic thwacking but rarely while buzzing with electric noise.
Hand trimming is slower so it means I can't trim every bush every
week. Maybe I should change my idea of how a bush should look.

This discussion is not really about musical instruments or hedges but an opportunity to consider the ways we go for the quick fix in our relationships and work, especially when it comes to managing our weakness. When we don't have answers, are books and conferences ways to engage the issues or technologies to avoid real engagement? When we feel overwhelmed by the needs of our congregations, are policies and programs technologies we use to predict and control outcomes? When we feel personally inadequate, does even our charm become a technology that lets us avoid real conversation? How in going for the quick fix do we do long-term damage to ourselves, our relationships and our churches?

Our culture is so encouraging of this avoidance of weakness that it takes some work to even remember it's an act. So let's challenge that culture by confessing the things that make us feel weak and how we try to avoid or fix our humanity. As a place to start, I offer my own weakness confessions (admitting that these only scratch the surface), hoping to make such confessions more common, less shameful.

Reflect

When you notice your limitations, how do you usually respond?

WHAT MAKES ME FEEL WEAK

While it's unfashionable and has been abused, scriptural confession allows us to see ourselves as part of a community of the broken. As you read my confessions, I invite you to shape yours. And share them.

Time. I have nothing beyond the here and now: my son sleeping in the room next to mine, my husband reading in the armchair, my dog waiting to be walked. These words ticking themselves out on this keyboard. My mind is clogged with regrets and memories past. My heart stands on tiptoe, leaning forward into an empty future. Will I have what it takes to send my daughter to college with freedom and courage?

Will I be with my parents when they die? If I am, will I just drop in for their final days? Maybe if we'd made better decisions in the past these wouldn't be our fears for the future. Or maybe there would be different fears. Maybe eighteen years ago . . . Maybe in six months . . .

My inability to change the past or predict the future makes me feel impotent. The surging desire to fix both meets with nothingness and I'm suspended here, in today.

> ### *Reflect*
> ---
> How do you feel about your inability to control the past and the future?

Understanding. Wanting to understand God is a good thing. Right up until when it's not.

No matter how I tell God what he could be teaching me right now, he doesn't take notice. And no matter how I order him to reveal himself in my timing, he seems uninterested. *I'm ready now, Lord! It would be really great if you could make all things known right now. Just explain what you're thinking and I'll accept it. Just reveal your ways and I'll know them.*

But if I'm honest, I'm not studying God for the sake of seeing something new; I'm trying to force him into the file drawers I already have. And he'll have none of it.

Until those moments when I'm asking for nothing, incapable of learning anything. Then he chooses to sweep in and blind me with insight, deafen me with his voice. A tiny bit of this would have been welcome at some other time, but now it's more than I can bear. When I finally do figure out what he's trying to tell me and how to make room for it in my life, it feels like a gift, like something to share with others.

And wanting to share God with others is a good thing. Right?

I see a place in someone else's life that looks like exactly where I was when God knocked the wind out of me. I want this moment to become a place of insight for her too. So I say, "Can we make a thing of this?" Like Peter at the transfiguration, I want to put up tabernacles. (Why am I so like the one who always missed the point?) I give action steps: "Just pray this prayer" or "Just set aside that unhealthy practice" or "Just name your fear" to lead my friend exactly to the place I've been. I set up flashing marquees, pave a road to it, fill the place with pillows, then find myself dragging my poor victim toward it, oblivious to the fact that the space I'm asking her to fill is shaped exactly like me.

Reflect

How do you seek understanding as a way to avoid weakness?

Parenting. My heart feels tender at risking to love something so fragile. And although these fragile creatures get stronger in their bodies, as they do they want to venture further away, wandering into relationships, ideas, websites! My discipline and example can do only so much, and beyond my limited control, my children have their own will. The question "Is God vulnerable?" seems ridiculous until I consider how it feels to love someone who may or may not love you back.[2] Then I know that, of any being, God is the most exposed to injury, over and over again—because of how much and how many he loves. To know that your love is the best thing for your beloved and to still let him or her choose whether to accept it makes you feel desperate. It makes me want to control, to force myself and my will on these naive things, to lecture them about all the possible dangers, to lock them away from harm. If I yell a little louder, they might see how serious I am, how scared I am.

Reflect

What family relationships make you feel vulnerable? Do you think God is vulnerable? If so, why?

Longing. When I was ten, I found a bird lying on my front steps. He drew my attention because, although the rest of him was completely still, he swatted his tail rhythmically on the concrete. It was unusual to see a kingfisher in the city, and as I knelt over him, I saw that something wasn't right. I filled a shoebox with grass, scooped him up and spent the rest of the day finding him bugs to eat and making him a tiny quilt, longing for him to get better and fly away. But all my efforts were in vain and by the end of the day he was only stillness. I was devastated, and my mother used up all her usual methods to calm me, finally letting me cry myself to sleep.

A few weeks later I came across a second bird on our front walkway (our cat had a nasty habit). I couldn't tell you what kind of bird it was or how it was injured because I didn't stop to look. To avoid the vulnerability of longing, I went to ask my father to bury it.

Letting myself want something without knowing if I'll ever get it makes me feel weak. Even longing for hope and love and God makes me feel vulnerable in this broken world because I get only glimpses. I believe God can do anything but I rarely see his power in its fullness. Living by generosity when all around me is scarcity makes me feel shaky.

If I just stop longing, stop looking, stop hoping, it will feel better. Or maybe if I just swamp my hope with instant gratification it will soothe the longing for now.

Reflect

What do you long for? Does longing make you feel vulnerable?

My body. This body of mine sends out feeble signals, wanting to give up right when I'm having a breakthrough, needing to sleep or eat right when the work is coming together. So weak, so needy. Get over it. Suck it up. We're on a deadline here, don't you know, wandering mind? People are counting on us, don't you know, gurgling stomach? We don't have time for feelings, failing heart! Only babies nap. Only wimps stay home when they're sick. Only losers say, "I can't do it." Override! Overcome!

We have ways of pushing through such weak, banal urges—medications, abusive self-talk, junk food. Time off is for sissies! Play is for children!

I have strong willpower. But my body can't keep up with my work ethic. Even when my feet ache, I can march myself right over a cliff. And I have. There's little to do in that place but look at your broken self. The inner drill sergeant has left in disgust and it's just you and your sad, feeble body, still quietly asking to rest, still needing to be fed. You have no choice but to live in this body because it's all you have. But now you live in it like you did as a child, eating, sleeping, relying on others for the important things.

Reflect

How do you feel the weakness of your body and what do you usually do about it?

WHAT DOESN'T MAKE ME FEEL WEAK (IN THE WRONG WAY)

Control, lovely control, is the best technology of all! It's all I need to avoid the messiness of parenting and intractability of time, the limitations of my body, my feelings, my understanding. To control how I look I just need to find the best products and procedures, be willing to devote time every day to preparation. It will take time and money but it will be worth it. I'll need to plan for the future because as I age it will take more time and money. I can budget for that.

To control what others think of me, I just need to read every book in my field as soon as it is released and read every book in my field that has ever been released and be able to quote extensively from them.

Which, of course, includes the Bible. I should know it by heart and be able to quote it at random on a regular basis. Controlling what others think of me means I only have to be up to date on all the pressing issues of the day and have a well-formulated, logically consistent response. All I have to do is be always ready to share my thoughts in a clear, entertaining and insightful way in written and spoken communication. All of this will also be very helpful in my efforts to control my own understanding. All that reading will surely come in handy when mysteries rear their ugly heads.

Other messy things that might need my attention can easily be taken care of with good old hard work, which never killed anyone. If I simply keep working until all the problems are solved, I'm guaranteed control! And if I make sure others keep working there will even be more productivity. When they complain, I'll just make a system. Their feelings, ideas and needs don't need to get in my way if we have policies and procedures and programs. When my own feelings threaten to undo me, I'll just set them aside.

Now it's time for a little fun! Never let it be said I can't have fun. A little partying, a little Internet, a lot of movies and those nasty, messy feelings just go away. Any guilt I feel about my neglect of my kids or any grief I feel that they will leave me one day seems to subside at the prospect of reality TV. (Look at those fools with all their problems! Their lives are so out of control.) And anyway, if any of these strategies lets me down, there's always prayer. I can just tell God everything I need. And it will be especially effective if I tell him he doesn't love me unless he gives it all to me.

Reflect

How will you confess your efforts to avoid weakness?

WHAT DOESN'T MAKE ME FEEL WEAK (IN THE RIGHT WAY)

There's plain old weakness. Then there's plain old control. But there's a third thing that I've yet to know how to name. It's when I'm aware of my smallness but there's no shame in it, no grappling for more but a peace in the immensity around me. I'm lost in it and at the same time found, not less for the lostness but larger. Enlarged not to become everything but to be a piece of everything, for everything to be in me. It happens when I sing with a crowd, whether in a choir or a stadium. I find it in the pool when I let myself be buoyed by the water and float aimlessly. I'm wrapped up in it when the creative process draws me into its dance. It meets me in prayer, where weakness has a voice. I've found it in ministry, on beaches and in storms. I've sat in the dark, watching a meteorite shower, feeling connected with the universe and all of history and at the same time being reminded of how it feels to read Scripture or be part of the church. There's something to this smallness! Something big!

It makes no sense that we can be saved by our smallness. It defies explanation that when we are lost we are found, when we are empty we are filled, when we are nothing we are part of everything. It's an uncomfortable truth that in losing control we find belonging. It takes courage to admit the technologies we've been using, to set them aside in favor of something we don't yet see in its fullness.

This may be the hardest and best thing you've ever done. But don't give up. If you're feeling a sense of your own smallness, and it's new and raw for you, be assured there is new hope to come. You may never feel strong again the way you did before—built up in confidence in yourself. But you can feel even stronger as you begin to see what you belong to, what wants to reveal itself in you.

What will your weakness confession be? And how will you share it? Are you willing to be the first to confess, to break the cycle of superhuman expectations and lead a culture of embracing what we are? When we take this risky step, we will be more fully ourselves and shape communities that know their need for God and for each other.

Reflect

Keep an ongoing weakness journal. How will you embrace the things that (in the right way) don't make you feel weak? How will you share that with others?

3

Save Me!

Vulnerability and Salvation

If we have been taught to mask our weakness, what does that mean for our salvation? We often base our relationship with God on our own understanding, on our feelings of his presence or on our own goodness. So our own ability becomes the foundation, which isn't much of a foundation at all. When we begin to fathom the depth of our inadequacy, we discover a firm foundation: our need for him.

I grew up trusting I was loved by my family and by God. Not because I was especially lovable but because I believed that my parents and God were capable of love. So when at age eleven I heard a sermon describing God's love as a gift and asking if we'd let it sit unopened or receive it, there was no question. Maybe as an eleven-year-old I was disturbed by the thought of an unopened gift, but I remember wanting to receive what God was offering me. The woman who prayed with me after that service said, "Mandy, I think God has something special for you." Since she was a missionary, my mind went straight to ministry.

In my teenage years, most of the adults trying to draw me and my fellow adolescents toward God assumed we felt far from him. My TV viewing at the time was limited to age-appropriate programming, so the most sordid stuff I heard came from the confessions of my youth leader, who shared his sins in an effort to get our attention and relate to all our pubescent sinfulness. I knew I made mistakes that made God unhappy but I still believed he was close. I began to feel left out at church because I wasn't wracked with guilt.

So I learned the spiritual discipline of wallowing. Every time I became aware of a sin I'd committed, I came to believe God was far from me, judging me until I fixed myself and made myself worthy of his presence again. And although I'd never experienced salvation in this way, I learned to evangelize by describing a gulf separating God from humanity, finishing the image by adding an awkward, cross-shaped bridge.

I remember the day in my twenties when I became aware of a way I'd been sinning, but this time, in the split second between rational recognition of the sin and the emotional wallowing, I caught myself thinking, "Oh, great, now I have to take the next two weeks feeling bad about myself and being totally unproductive to show I'm repentant."

Scripture talks about our guilty state, not a need for guilty feelings. So in that moment I made the radical choice just to ask for forgiveness, trust that God would give it and change my actions. I chose to take all the energy I usually invested in guilty self-loathing and invest it instead in growth, which was a good thing.

But again, it left me on the outside of most conversations I heard about salvation. I had never actively rejected God, never made a conscious choice to stray from him. So I had never really chosen to return to him. Was I really saved? What had he saved me from? And to? Even after getting a biblical studies degree, I could explain the difference between propitiation and redemption, but could I tell a story of it? Did I feel redeemed? I wished I had a story like others—of drug use and crime that brought me to rock bottom and the life change that came about when I accepted Jesus. When I remembered "my decision," I remembered more of an affirmation than a conversion.

But there were those words to cling to: "God has something special for you."

And somewhere along the way I started adding the words "to do."

If the special thing he had for me was to share his love with others through ministry, then I would do it with all my might. I did it with all my might by working to get awards and scholarships in college. I did it with all my might by being the best Bible college professor's wife, the best freelance writer, the best at-home mother I could be. And when the kids started school, I did it with all my might by being the best part-time associate pastor I could be.

I would get all my tasks done and then invent new ones. I would not only maintain the systems I oversaw, I would improve them. When it wore me out or discouraged me, I would keep my complaining or my tears to myself. Something deep inside me sensed that something wasn't right. I called it tiredness or stress and set it aside, did what perfectionists and performers do—pushed through it so no one would see how scared and small I was. I was here to be the nicest and most efficient representation of God's love anyone had ever seen.

After all, God had something special for me (to do). I was good at my job. And people who are good at their jobs keep getting more responsibilities. So it was with me. And with each unfolding of leadership, I shouldered the new load as a burden and soldiered on through the anxiety.

Until that moment at that conference. At the time it raised doubts about my ability to do ministry. But in hindsight I've learned that God was also working on a deeper level—the foundation of my relationship with him. Given how I had come to understand my salvation, my failure to be good enough in ministry undermined my entire faith. When I found that I actually couldn't do the special thing God had for me (to do), it was failure like I'd never felt, emptiness like I'd never known. I had no energy left to keep up the facade I had created and it crumbled, revealing a discouraged, naked soul. A soul still loved by God but of no use for doing special things.

As you know, that exposure among such shiny people sent me running for my hotel room. But not without drawing the attention of a woman from the prayer room down the hall. She offered to pray with me and, comforted by the presence of another human being, I accepted. As she prayed she broke into tongues, something my tradition has never been comfortable with. The rational side of me kept saying, *We don't believe in this. This is weird.* But all the while my broken heart understood perfectly. She made the sounds a mother dove makes as she folds her wing around her young—a place to protect nakedness, to be not terribly special. A place of grace.

My body eventually moved on from that prayer room, but for the next day my spirit remained under its care. Although I mourned for all the special things I could never do for God, I felt no shame. Deep loss, absolute emptiness, but no shame. That love I'd had since childhood was with me still, in this place that felt like a tomb. All I had tried to be was dying but whatever was left of me was loved by God.

I see now that he could still love what was left of me because his understanding of human limitation is not a theoretical one. The same God who wept when Lazarus died was weeping with me. The God in the garden who begged to be released from torture sat with me. And although I didn't yet see it, the God who showed himself stronger than all human suffering was also there. He was unafraid of my weakness. And yet he felt distant, his words of reassurance vague. I longed for him to feel closer, but in hindsight I wonder if he was holding back because dancing would have been inappropriate.

As much as he saw my pain, it was hard for him to mourn with me. He knew what was breaking but he also knew the way he could redeem it. It was hard for him not to rejoice at the things I was allowing to die there—control, perfection, performance. It felt to me like a great loss because I'd held on to those things for so long. But he knew what would fill the void they left—a deep reliance on him.

Whatever confidence in myself I was losing would make room for confidence in him. Whatever gaping emptiness I was for the first time perceiving would create space for him to fill. I had finally stopped doing special things long enough to allow him to give me the special thing he had for me—himself.

This is where my journey stopped being about help from God to do my job and started being about salvation. Over and over the psalmist cries out for salvation, and it's difficult to distinguish if he longs for salvation from adversaries who lust after his blood or for salvation from his own lusts. Paul begs for release from his thorn in the flesh, and we don't know if he is hounded by a physical limitation, an insecurity or the weighty memory of his history as a persecutor. Or maybe he calls for release from an insatiable appetite for sin. In every case our Father longs to be the one we cry out to. If our sin is any way we fall short of his glory, that covers *every* way we are human and in need of him.

We often see sin as a consequence of our own choices, a place where God will not come to our aid. Tough love and consistency are great in parenting, helping us avoid the kind of hovering that cushions our children from real life. But this kind of parenting makes us believe that if our weakness comes from a choice we made, then as far as our tough-love Father is concerned, we're on our own. If our weakness grows from our choices, from an insatiable hunger we have indulged or a sinful distraction we cannot shake, what right do we have to ask for God's help? We got ourselves into this mess; we should get ourselves out. As Brennan Manning puts it,

> The American church today accepts grace in theory but denies it in practice. . . . We believe that we can pull ourselves up by our bootstraps—indeed, we can do it ourselves. Sooner or later we are confronted with the painful truth of our inadequacy and insufficiency. Our security is shattered and our bootstraps are

cut. . . . Our huffing and puffing to impress God, our scrambling for brownie points, our thrashing about trying to fix ourselves while hiding our pettiness and wallowing in guilt are nauseating to God and are a flat out denial of the gospel of grace.[1]

Even the most consistent parent, when his child steps into oncoming traffic, does not lecture his bleeding child and say, "I told you not to run into the street; you'll just have to lie there and experience the consequences of your choices." No, the parent whisks that child to the hospital and leaves the lectures for later. If we as weak and human parents can give grace to our disobedient children, how much more can God's grace step in, even when we're wracked with our own lusts and temptations, even when we do that thing we don't want and we don't do that thing we do want?[2]

Reflect

Do you ever find yourself believing that your sin is your own problem to fix? Even if your choices got you into it, how can you ask for God's help out of it?

When Paul begged for his thorn to be removed, God's response was, "My grace is sufficient for you, for my power is made perfect in weakness" (2 Corinthians 12:9). This is not plastic perfection. This is fullness, God's grace having room to expand to its full measure, God's power having space the more we are empty. Mountaineer Joe Simpson tells his chilling story in the book and movie *Touching the Void*.[3] Thousands of feet up the side of the Siula Grande mountain, Joe's safety line was cut, leaving Joe to slide with a broken leg into a deep crevasse. After several desperate attempts to climb up and out of the crevasse, he was faced with the fact that his injury made it impossible. And so, against all survival instinct, he made the excruciating choice to lower himself deeper into the crevasse in the hope that there would be other exits farther down, all the time wondering, "Am I lowering myself to freedom or deeper into the belly of the earth? Does a ray of sunlight await me in the pit, showing a way out into day, or is there only darkness and slow death?" With every inch he lowered himself down, he edged farther from the obvious way to life—and there was no way back up.

Our understanding of salvation often begins with the image of a chasm separating us from God.[4] It's a meaningful image for many people, but it doesn't ring true with my own experience. Instead, what has gnawed at me is the sense of my own emptiness. Instead of space between me and God, I've always felt space between what I am and what I should be. When we look inside ourselves and see how far we are from fullness, we set our sights on the brim, way above, and scrabble up the sides of the crevasse to reach it. Trying every skill, every kind of intellect, every ounce of will and might, we inch upward, but before long we become aware of the brokenness in us and have no choice but to admit that we're getting nowhere. We can go on with this our whole lives, exhausting every resource in our desperate effort to ascend.

Or we can stop. We can realize that even what we think we have accomplished is not possible without the breath in our lungs, the current in our nerves, the gifts, the opportunities, the intellect that comes from him. Whatever we thought we were offering God to reach whatever meager completeness we think we can achieve—it's still all him. We're children buying gifts for our Father from the allowance he has given us.

It's here that we are faced with a new, sickening and yet invigorating possibility. What if, instead of this futile effort to inch into the pretense of fullness, we made a counterintuitive, countercultural choice? What if we chose to lower ourselves, to defy every survival instinct and start emptying? It almost breaks us to make that choice, to switch from what feels like sensible self-preservation to an act that will drain us.

Are we emptying to our own death? Will there be anything left of us? What will we find at the bottom? Will it be the horror and darkness of the pit? When we find ourselves empty, looking up at the void of all we are not, will we see only what is lacking or will we discover we have created a greater space for God to fill, a place for his strength to be made complete? When we find nothing but an echoing chamber over us, will we fill it up with cries for our Father?

> ### Reflect
> ---
> What would emptying look like for you? How might it create space for God to show his fullness?

Acts 2:21 says, "Everyone who calls on the name of the Lord will be saved." What if belief were not so much intellectual assent to a set of doctrines but following a gut-level instinct to call out for help? Belief would become living in dependence, which then would teach us to believe. In whatever way we are able to perceive our lack and call out to our Father, he is faithful to make us complete. And that feels like the gospel.

How we have experienced the gospel is inextricable from how we share it. If our salvation is walled up with arguments, it's only natural that we will try to argue people into it. If it's carefully constructed out of doctrinal statements, it makes sense that we evangelize by providing a carefully arranged list of ideas. Those feel like very strong positions from which to expand our empire. But if our need for a Savior comes from a sense of our own weakness, how can we have it all together enough to share it with anyone? Is it our job to be spiritually sufficient or to show how God is sufficient?

After twenty years in ministry I'm still waiting to see the kinds of conversions I've heard preachers talk about. Some amalgam of all the evangelists from all the revivals I've ever attended has looked over my shoulder, watching my score. So when Shannon, a UCC member, asked me to lead a prayer group with two of her friends who wouldn't call themselves Christians, I knew this was my opportunity to "practice" on them. Together Shannon and I met with these two incredibly spiritual women—Karenna, a yoga instructor with an eclectic approach to spirituality, and Cathy, who had been raised by atheist Jewish nature lovers and was exploring how to make God a part of her life.

We had some of the best conversations I've ever had about God. When you get together with a group of Christians, you don't often stop to define who or what God is—an energy or a being with a will and a personality? Although we didn't agree on all areas of theology, when we prayed together, something united us. To this day those prayers are some of the most powerful I have ever enjoyed. As the pastor in the room, it became my job to end the prayer each week and I always ended with "In Jesus' name, Amen," which felt very Christian.

As I look back on our conversations, I cringe as I remember my efforts to explain Jesus. At one point Cathy raised the question we were all feeling: "We have so much in common, but some of us have this extra Jesus part and some don't. So what difference does Jesus make?"

This was what I'd prayed for and I felt my performance anxiety switch into gear. I hoped to convince them of something true—but I didn't even convince myself. I was still learning myself the difference Jesus makes. I can only pray that while my explanation was less than memorable, they still carry with them the ways I lived the difference Jesus makes, even ways I couldn't verbalize myself. While part of my motivation in joining the prayer group had been to "fix" people, along the way I found that I myself needed a prayer group. As strange as it felt, I allowed them to minister to me and I pray that in it God somehow ministered to them.

You may have noticed that I referred to these wonderful women as "people who wouldn't call themselves Christians." The reason for this phrase is that my ministry team decided we would use the term "non-Christian" only among Christians. Certainly Scripture makes references to outsiders, but these references are found in letters written to Christians. We do of course agree that there is something distinct that defines us as Christians—the "Christ" part. But to talk in terms of "Christian" and "non-Christian" to a non-Christian audience is to lay over their experience a value system they do not hold and to set them outside of us. They would certainly not self-identify as Christians, but would they call themselves "non-Christians"?

Part of my team's decision was about being sensitive to the fact that defining others negatively isn't the best way to begin a conversation. But the more pressing issue for me is a concern that creating a wall in our language might create a barrier for them, especially if they see themselves almost as part of us. If they are experiencing their discovery of Jesus as a gradual process and we divide it neatly into black and white with a big wall dividing the two, will we set them further away from Jesus than we want? Further away from Jesus than they think they are?

I no longer spend a lot of time plotting people along that spectrum of "very, very Christian" to "very, very non-Christian." When I've done that, it's surprised me to find that God has burrowed tunnels from one section of the spectrum to another. When I've done that, my comments to "non-Christians" have suddenly revealed that I saw them as foreigners from another land, and just when they were about to ask to move in, they instead decided to retreat to that foreign land. In short, my efforts to decide where people are on the "spectrum" have underestimated God's work in their lives.

I'm learning from people like Nathan Lutz, founder of the TOAG (Training for Ordinary Apprentices to Go) internship program, that sharing good news involves a vulnerable submission to the process.

His description of his work with unreached people groups goes against all the usual tactics:

> Whenever we reverted back to our old evangelism tactic, we watched the resistance build; arguments followed and doors closed. When we did not try to convince them of truth but merely declared our love for God and why we loved him, they were much more open to discover truth on their own. . . . The refreshing possibility is that with this approach, people can be discipled into the kingdom rather than being called to make a decision they are not ready to make. They can enter a process of discovery. Jesus chose to disciple his disciples until they believed; the Western church is bent on trying to disciple people who have hardly believed but made some kind of decision.[5]

So at UCC we spend a lot of effort learning to dance wherever God is. Any point of clarity we find, any sign of goodness, any experience of his presence we paint and talk and write and sing about. Alan Hirsch and Michael Frost's writing about centered and bounded sets has helped us in this. As an Aussie, I love their metaphor, which is taken from the Australian Outback: On huge farms in Australia where the livestock roam over hundreds of miles, the farmers don't need to build fences but instead, in that arid landscape, they keep their animals close by digging wells.[6] We spend a lot of energy digging wells, and it's beginning to show life.

The more I have tried to share good news by convincing people, arguing my points, creating thoroughly consistent systems, the more deflated I've felt. Instead of the interest I hoped to spark in people's faces, I've seen defensiveness, annoyance and boredom. On the other hand, the more we work at telling stories of lived theology and invite people to watch firsthand our experience of and reliance on God, the more they come to see his power. But to let his power be shown through our reliance on him, we may end up sharing the gospel through our own need, which rarely feels good. So we question its rightness.

We love getting to the conversion. We love it because we get to see Jesus at work in people's hearts. But maybe we also love it because we changed someone or got our way. Our evangelism method became a device to force a quick fix. Do we leave room for God to work in the hearts of others, or is it our job to map out every step of their journey? Storyteller Joe Boyd creates events where Bible stories can stand on their own two feet outside of church buildings. It is an evangelistic act, but he admits that he's done with the usual methods of evangelism:

> I get tired of that pressure we put on people to change their worldview. If it's supposed to happen, it will happen through the Spirit and the Word. I've released myself from the pressure to do that for people. . . . There's such power in story. . . . When you're hearing a story and you're into it, your brain isn't wired to have a counterpoint. . . . When someone comes to our events, they can decide for themselves if it's myth or propaganda, but the important thing is that they hear the story. . . . Have we lost the foundational skill of just standing up and telling a story?[7]

In recent years, permission- and friendship-based approaches have become preferred methods of evangelism.[8] It's been good to move away from the quick-fix evangelism technologies of the past. But when we get permission and make friends, in the moment when Jesus most wants to reveal himself through us, does he reveal only his resurrected, glorified, resolved self? Or will we also allow him to come to humanity through us in the way he chose to come to humanity originally—as a human? Are we willing to allow the divine to be revealed by our not being divine? Rather than sharing our strong ideas or morals, are we willing to reveal our need for God's strength?

Are our stories of salvation distant memories or ongoing stories of reliance on God? Are they stories of the moment we checked off a list of doctrines? Or are they stories of a moment we came to understand with our whole selves? Are they stories of knowing all the answers and having superhuman strength? Or are they stories of a dying Jesus who met us when we felt like dying?

> If we really believe the gospel we proclaim, we'll be honest about our own beauty and brokenness, and the beautiful broken One will make himself known to our neighbors through the chinks in our armor—and in theirs.
>
> **Fil Anderson**[9]

Beyond telling, are we willing to let others watch our stories even as they happen? Even the messy, confusing parts so that we're no longer the storyteller but the character in a drama God is weaving? I personally can't tell you a salvation story of far-from-to-close-to-God. But I can tell you a salvation story of death-to-life. I remember a tomb and I know the life that began there.

Reflect

What is the story of your need for God?

4

Feeling Exposed

How Vulnerable Pastors Handle Emotions

> *In short, life is fundamentally about emotion.*
> *If you do not attune to it, you will eventually respond to it*
> *anyway, but in forms of thought, feeling, and behavior*
> *that bring you closer to shame than glory.*
>
> CURT THOMPSON, *ANATOMY OF THE SOUL*

It's an odd thing to break into tears while chairing an elders' meeting. Before our gathering I'd done my homework and had all the facts we needed to make decisions. But when we came to an agenda item about staffing, I became overwhelmed by my feelings—care for the staff person involved, worries that I had failed, fear about financial ramifications. I bit my lip to control my tears, but that has never really worked. With embarrassment I discovered I had brought the meeting to a standstill. But my tears revealed the complexity of the issue and (once I stopped apologizing) the conversation took on a new dimension.

There are few things that make us feel more vulnerable than our own emotions. Anger, fear, sadness all knock us off our feet right when we're trying to look like leaders. If we have been told that leadership is always strong, how do we respond to this breaking in of emotion?

Is emotion something to control or does it reveal opportunities for God to show himself?

Last week I was part of a workshop on understanding poverty. We heard heartbreaking stories: parents working long hours but unable to make ends meet, dreaming of change but stuck in old cycles. Afterward the facilitator asked, "How does this make you feel?" I wondered whether people would say "sad," "frustrated" or "angry." All I could think was "heavy."

But the answers given were not about feelings. The first response was, "I think that happened to those people because . . . " And the second: "That reminds me of . . . "

I was still frustrated by that conversation when we watched a video about empathy by Brené Brown.[1] In it she says, "Empathy fuels connection; sympathy drives disconnection. . . . Empathy is feeling with people. . . . Empathy is a choice. It's a vulnerable choice because in order to connect with you I have to connect with something in myself that knows that feeling." On the other hand, she says, the sympathetic response changes the subject or tries to fix the problem. This seemed ironic right after the two responses that had changed the subject and tried to fix the problem. If we want to connect, we need empathy, which requires us to connect with our own feelings. Which does not always feel great.

As I reflected on the experience, I realized that the two unsatisfying responses were from men, and I jumped to conclusions: "Typical men! Out of touch with their emotions. Always wanting to look strong and in control." But before the day was over I was humbled. While hearing a church member's story of family abuse, I had the same "fix it" response: "Well, what you need to do is . . . " Her problem was messy and I wanted to clean it up—quickly, before I felt something.

We've been sold a lot of stories about gender and emotion. (Women are emotional. Men are not.) We've also been sold a lot of stories about gender and power. (Women are weak. Men are strong.) And we've been sold a lot of stories about emotion and power. (Emotion is weakness. So powerful leaders should be in control of their emotions or, better yet, have none.) But these stories don't leave much room for human hearts. Our culture has shaped what it means to be a man, which in turn has shaped what it means to be a leader, which in turn has shaped what it means for women to lead. These expectations are burdensome for all of us—men and women. So to learn human kinds of leadership, it's important for us to look at gender and emotion.

Early in my preaching ministry I had a conversation with a nationally known preacher whose advice could be summed up as, "Be totally yourself . . . but don't be too much of a woman." I understand that it will get old if all my sermon illustrations come from pregnancy, but he could have just said, "Be sure you relate to your audience"— good advice for men *and* women. What it affirmed to me was the unspoken message I'd heard my whole life—if you want to be taken seriously by a mixed audience, hold off on the emotional stuff.

We often try to overcome emotion with strength. Well, feeble efforts at it. Whether we're faced with the complexity of poverty or the heartbreak of divorce or the fear of looking foolish, emotion upsets our equilibrium, sometimes suddenly. Tears look weak. Admissions such as "That hurt me" or "I'm overwhelmed by that question" or "I'm embarrassed by this situation" look weak. But anger, argument and ready answers don't. So when we're trying to look strong and emotion hits, we desperately do whatever makes it seem to go away. Most of the time, however, what we've actually done is defer it or transfer our hurt to someone else. The quick fix turns into a kind of violence as we transform our raw emotion into disconnection and a subtle form of abuse.

Susan Scott, a conversational consultant, uses the image of an "emotional wake," which implies that we leave something behind with every conversation—something for which we should take responsibility. "It can be an afterglow, aftertaste, or aftermath," she says.[2] For leaders, an emotional wake of control is more socially acceptable than one of admitting limitations. It feels good to act out recklessly rather than face our emotions, but in the long run it takes more energy to mop up the mess. And it misses the opportunity to engage well with each other and with God.

I've tried pretending I have no emotions, but not only is it untrue to who I am, it's untrue to who we all—men and women—really are as humans. It continues the stereotype that half my congregation and half my staff have no emotion (or shouldn't). It buys in to falsehoods: to be a leader is to be like a man and to be like a man is to be emotionless. If, regardless of gender, we can learn to be comfortable with our emotion, to take responsibility for it and express it in a way that respects others' emotions, we will find a way to be whole humans. As I figure out how to be emotionally present in my leadership, I've watched the men I lead find courage to face their own feelings.[3] This is not a gender-specific issue. Our freedoms are intertwined as women and men.

Here's why this is important: we have been told that emotion is weakness and we have also been told that there is no place for weakness in leadership. So how can any of us as emotional beings find a way to lead?

We have talked for years about the expectations our culture creates for women, but we are beginning to see what unrealistic expectations we also have for men—that they be strong and in control at all times. Child psychologists Dan Kindlon and Michael Thompson have devoted their careers to studying the ways we raise boys. They believe that "our culture is railroading boys into lives of isolation, shame and anger" and have found that "boys, beginning at a young age, are systematically steered away from their emotional lives toward silence, solitude, and distrust."[4]

A video by the Representation Project called *The Mask You Live In* explores why, compared to girls, "boys in the U.S. are more likely to be diagnosed with a behavior disorder, prescribed stimulant medications, fail out of school, binge drink, commit a violent crime, and/or take their own lives." This video, which begins with a litany of messages we tell our boys—"Stop crying!" "Be cool!" "Be a man!"—goes on to quote psychologist and educator Niobe Way: "They really buy into a culture that doesn't value what we have feminized. If you're in a culture that doesn't value caring, doesn't value relationships, doesn't value empathy, you are going to have boys and girls, men and women go crazy."[5]

As it took courage for me to create my own way to lead, it will take courage for men to step out of the pressure to always be in control. It will take wives and mothers who are willing to let their husbands and sons be human. It will take brothers and fathers who choose not to play macho head games with each other. Not only will this bring about freedom for men, it will affect us all as we redefine human leadership and what it means to be emotional beings who also lead.

A poem that made the rounds during the women's movement still resonates today:

For every woman who is tired of being called "an emotional female," there is a man who is denied the right to weep and to be gentle. . . .

For every woman who takes a step toward her own liberation, there is a man who finds the way to freedom has been made a little easier.[6]

I've been in the "men have created the problem that oppresses me" camp, but I'm coming to see that we all suffer for society's superhuman (or subhuman) norms of emotional control. This is not about men's rights versus women's rights. We need each other to work this out. We may never be comfortable with the particular emotions we feel, but when we can resign ourselves to the vulnerability of emotion, we will find new ways to connect with each other and with God.

How a leader handles his or her own emotions will shape the culture of the church. When the leader is self-aware and communicates emotion well, this has the potential to create an incredibly healthy church and staff culture.[7] Ignoring emotion doesn't mean it has no effect on our culture, just that the effect is indirect and reactionary instead of proactive and purposeful. As Peter Scazzero puts it, "The overall health of any church or ministry depends primarily on the emotional and spiritual health of its leadership. In fact, the key to successful spiritual leadership has much more to do with the leader's internal life than with the leader's expertise, gifts, or experience."[8]

For me, this has meant being okay with my own sensitivity, working out the patterns of what hurts and overwhelms me, figuring out how to explain my feelings to others. It means I have to wrestle with baggage from my background and the culture, forgive others, forgive myself and just let a lot of stuff go. It's a lot of work. I process with God every day, with a friend every week, with a counselor every month. I journal and talk through my emotions to work out how to explain them to myself and others.

But wholeness does not mean resolving all emotion. Wholeness

> A leader must separate his or her own emotional being from that of his or her followers while still remaining connected. Vision is basically an emotional rather than a cerebral phenomenon, depending more on a leader's capacity to deal with anxiety than his or her professional training or degree.
>
> **Edwin H. Friedman**[9]

comes from embracing what makes us human, acknowledging that emotion is normal and naming and releasing it. It's an ongoing struggle. But it's comforting to know it's not only my struggle. To remind you it's not only your struggle, let me continue this act of confession by sharing some of the emotions I work to understand and live into well.

DARKNESS

Before we talk about depression I should make something clear. I can see how this "Any weakness is a ministry resource" idea could become "If I'm worn out or depressed, I should see it as more ministry opportunity and just keep working." But as we grow in comfort with our own weaknesses, we begin to learn what is normal and what is a sign of something serious that needs attention. We need to trust professionals and loved ones to help us see the difference. Please don't see my thoughts on depression as professional advice. I share my story of depression to alleviate our shame.

Our culture sees depression as the ultimate failure: you can't accomplish anything anymore, so what's the point of you? When humans are valued based on their productivity, what value do we have when we no longer fulfill a function? The shame of losing our role as a cog in the machine means depression is often kept quiet. And medicated. I have taken antidepressant medications. I would like to honestly say I have no shame about that.

I don't want to say depression is a friend (the ideal is to recover from it), but I've learned that depression is a forced sabbath, just as physical illness can be, a time when we have no choice but to rest. The shame and anxiety ("I shouldn't be depressed" and "How long will this depression last?") take energy away from healing. Nature has built-in failsafe switches. Just as a woman is physically unable to reproduce when she is seriously ill—her system shuts down nonessential functions to funnel energy into recovery—in the same way, when our hearts are breaking, they shut down all nonessential functions to focus on healing. And so one of the best ways to embrace weakness is to take permission to rest our hearts.

A few years ago I spoke these words: "I don't want to die. I just don't want to live for a while."

Within minutes of hearing this sobering admission from me, my mum booked a flight to be with me for a month. For a while she helped me live—packing lunches, washing towels. I had taken on too much responsibility for the running of the world and, for a month at least, I was released to just be.

One night during this time I trudged upstairs to bed with the sense that there was still one more task for my exhausted mind before blessed sleep. It disturbed me to realize that the task I dreaded was the process of reading and praying myself into God's presence. With every step around our spiral staircase my mind took a new turn, and I remember the exact step where I swore off my devotions. I had given the physical work to my mother and I would give the spiritual work to my Father.

In my heart I knew that I read and prayed every night not to make God close but to make myself aware of his closeness. But gaining that awareness took a lot of work: putting off the cares of the day, focusing on the truths of Scripture, journaling, praying without wandering or snoozing. Wouldn't it be easier to just stop and be aware of his closeness? So every night for a month I brushed my teeth, turned out the light and just basked for a bit. I didn't say anything or ask him to say anything. I just trusted that he was there, that he was good, that he loved me and that that was enough. The darkness all around me was God. The silence was God. The sleep was God.

After my month I resurrected some of my more structured spiritual disciplines. But they were different. I did them for a new reason and with more creativity because I'd had a monthlong holiday with my Father. And just as my mum and I reminisce now about that month we shared life together, even still my Father and I draw from those shared experiences. And I've become okay with living again.

Reflect

How do you experience times of darkness?

GRIEF

Moving internationally three times in my life has meant many tearful goodbyes. So with every major event in the lives of any of the hundred people I love in other parts of the world, I'm aware that I'm not sharing it with them. With every major event in my life, I notice the quiet of the space they're not filling beside me. Every Christmas, wedding, birth carries a layer of grief. Cards in the mail aren't quite the same as a warm body.

Living near the Bible college where my husband, Jamie, teaches brings its own grief. We chose our location so we could invest in the lives of his students and we regularly have them in our home, advising them on major life choices, attending their weddings and ordinations and then sending them off. Every single year. The neighborhood shifts from bustling with life to deadly quiet very suddenly every May. In addition to that, one hill over our church and my job are in a different, bigger campus setting. We regularly send people out from there as well. Not only do we have to say goodbye, we have to send our friends well, praying them on their way, rejoicing, organizing gifts and farewell events.

It gets old, this life of constant emptying. It would be easier to stop caring, stop building relationships with new students or investing in new church members. They're just going to leave anyway, so why bother?

The only thing that makes me feel a little better is talking to the only One who never will leave. And trusting that that constant One is also with my loved ones, far from me.

Reflect

How do you experience grief?

DOUBT

I rarely start my day asking, "Is my relationship with my husband real?

What if I've just imagined that I love him? Is it safe to trust that he loves me?" And I rarely start my day thinking, "Exactly what is the rate of my husband's hair growth? Why does he like chocolate cold and hard when obviously warm and melty is the best? If I don't know these things about him, how close can we really be?"

Instead, he hands me my morning cup of tea and I ask him how he slept. And our day begins.

People often tell me, "I'm just not feeling God right now. Could you ask someone else to pray? It seems inauthentic if I say things I don't feel." Or, "I'm really struggling with what I think about [fill in the blank], and it seems hypocritical to come to Sunday services when I don't know what I believe."

We hold ideals of how and what we should feel—God is close, God loves us, we are precious in his sight. And we hold ideals of how and what we should believe—knowing our position on every theological and cultural issue and having our arguments thoroughly proof-texted. But when we have such high ideals for what faith looks like, how do we get on with the process of living this life of faith? Especially when human feelings and understanding can be so fickle?

Maybe there's a third option: just doing. Faithfulness in my marriage doesn't mean I always feel mushy feelings. It doesn't mean I fully understand my husband's physical, mental or emotional inner workings. And yet I am faithful by living life with him, raising these children together, getting up each morning to tea and small talk. And in the midst of that there are the gifts of warm feelings and moments of insight into his mysteries.

Why are we okay with that elusive quality in our human relationships but not in our relationship with God? Christians have community rituals, but what about personal and family practices that remain constant when feelings and understanding come and go? I see Christians exerting a lot of energy managing their doubt and persevering through the darkness of God's distance. I admire their good intentions but I also see how it wears them out. It depletes self-control, a resource that we have in limited supply and that could be better used in other ways. Instead, the rituals and regular rhythms of individual and family life—whether it's regular sabbath practices, times of prayer throughout our days, weekly commitments to acts of service—can help make our faith more of a doing and less of a feeling or thinking. There is still room for emotional highs and moments of intellectual clarity, but they come without being forced. And when they do, they're seen as a blessing, not a requirement.[10]

If you watched me in my ministry it would be easy to think I always feel God's presence or always feel sure of my beliefs. I don't. But after years of frustration, wanting to feel more or know more, I have given up the constant monitoring of the close to/far from God spectrum and the doubt/belief gauge. Instead I pray at the beginning of meetings and sing the doxology at the end of services because that's just what we do. I don't do them because I always understand or feel them. I do them because I trust with a belief deeper than thought and a sense deeper than feeling that they are true even though my feelings and understanding come and go.[11]

Reflect

How do you wrestle with doubt?

FRUSTRATION

To get to know a class of Bible college students recently, I asked them their names and their plans after college. They set their faces as they took turns reciting the familiar scripts. I saw their discomfort, so I apologized and started again. "Let me ask this instead: What frustrates you in the world and what would you like to do about it?"

The air in the room changed and answers began to flow easily. It was no longer a question of performance but of passion. Students shared, "I'm frustrated when inner city kids have to raise themselves. I want to encourage them." And "Because of my own family history, I'm frustrated that addicts often struggle alone. I want to be with them."

Frustration doesn't always feel like a Christian motivation—we're supposed to be content in all circumstances. But prophets were frustrated. Jesus was frustrated. The apostles were frustrated. And so I've embraced it. My frustration began because the church was too interwoven with the world. Then I became frustrated that the church was too detached from the world. It made me read, ask questions. When I couldn't find answers, my frustration drove me to wrestle with God. And to look for every possible way forward, for every ally—on the radio, in nature, in novels, in Scripture, in music and movies, in my own story and the stories of my friends. When I saw they had some of the same frustrations, I realized these were good frustrations.

Frustration comes from high ideals—a desire to see justice or meaning or hope, to see God's children know his love, to see the church run unhindered. Frustration motivates us to fight for our ideals even when it seems pointless. Frustration with infertility drives parents to endure the obstacles to adoption. Frustration with bad theology gives professors the patience to answer the same questions every single semester. Frustration with voicelessness reshapes itself into new ways of communicating. Frustration with cancer leads to the development of new treatments. Frustration with the failings of our own parents makes us strive to be better parents. Frustration makes the Lord's Prayer no longer a singsongy "kingdom-come, will-be-done" rhyme but a cry for heaven to show itself on earth. Frustration gives us no choice but to call out to God to aid our efforts, to join our cause. Frustration grows from our longing. And our longing connects us to a God who longs to be known.

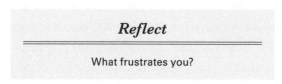

Reflect

What frustrates you?

DISCOMFORT

The café run by our church forces us regularly into situations that give me a stomachache. Since it's a center of the university community, students love hanging out and holding events here. At one point Dylan, a regular from the university's sexuality studies department, wanted to host a panel discussion, and our café seemed like a natural choice to her. However, while we wanted to welcome Dylan as a person, we were aware that the conversation at this public event might be pretty explicit sexually. And we were committed to making our public art, music and events in the café "family friendly." So we wrote back and politely told her that her event wouldn't work with our "family friendly" policy.

There was email silence for a week from Dylan and then we received a passionate response. She had read "family friendly" not in the way we had meant it (that is, "PG-rated") but through the political "family values" lens. But rather than anger (I'm guessing the week of email silence had allowed her to deal first with that), she responded with pleading. She told us about her own family and described the families of others involved in the event, asking, "Are we not families?" If we had set out to define what a family was or was not and she had not liked it, we would have had to deal with that. But that's not what we meant to do, and she was responding from her misunderstanding.

As I read her email, a knot slowly grew in my stomach. We had stepped into a mess. While I don't believe we had done anything "wrong," we had inadvertently hurt someone. I wanted the stomach knot to go away, but all night long it just tightened. I tossed around in my bed, flipping from a desire to be understood ("Why would she not give us the benefit of the doubt? We didn't mean it that way!") to defensiveness ("Here we are, trying to share our building and ourselves with the community! No one knows how much it costs us physically, emotionally, financially. All we do is give and she attacks us?") to dismissiveness ("It's just going to get ugly if we respond so maybe we should just let it go.").

All of these were quick fixes to make me feel better about the growing knot. But eventually, in the middle of this sleepless night, I decided I had to respond from my knottedness. I set aside my politely defensive email drafts and wrote:

> I want to write to apologize and tell you how distressed I am by how we made you feel.
>
> We are still learning how to share this space well and, to be honest, it's one of the most humbling things we've ever stepped into! True engagement in diversity is messier than we even knew! But it's what we feel called to even though we're not good at it yet.
>
> We are still developing our policies and had not thought about how "family-friendly" would sound to you. We meant it more along the lines of "for a general audience" and I am deeply disturbed that you felt it was a judgment of your family. I know how "family-friendly" or "family values" have been politicized (often by Christians) but didn't think about it in that light here and I want you to know that was not our intention. . . .
>
> I cannot say how deeply disturbed I am by how we came across to you. My deepest longing as pastor of this place is that the people of this community would know they are loved, by us and by God. I fear we have done the opposite here and it breaks my heart. All

I can say is sorry. I don't know if you will still want to be in our space but let me assure you that every single member of this church community would consider you to be made in the image of God.

It took all I had at 3 a.m. to write this, and yet it felt strangely good to have permission not to fix the problem. Surprisingly, though, in some ways it did fix the problem. Dylan saw my heart, saw that I connected to her as a human. When she responded to this email she finished by saying, "This is one of the few times in my life that I feel like activism, education and honesty have played out perfectly." She had shared earlier that these were some of her highest values, so, for her, this represented a significant exchange. It represented some of my highest values as well because it was one of the few times in what could have become a ballistic situation that I have seen grace, transparency and empathy played out. I hope it might help begin to heal something our culture has broken. And I hope to continue our conversation in person.

Beginning my day this way awoke a new place in my heart. I saw the power present in sinking feelings, how dread in the pit of my stomach could fuel creativity and community, how complicated questions could open doors to a slow process of relationship building if we resisted the urge to reach for the quick fix. I felt alive to my own emotion and raw, yet strangely empowered.

As I drove home that afternoon, I stopped at the intersection where I always stop, the one where there is always a homeless person with a sign. Usually I see this person and feel inadequate. The need is so much more complicated than I can solve with a drive-by handout.

The inadequacy usually makes me turn away, and I daresay the person at that corner sees little but the backs of heads. This time, as I pulled up to the lights, a young woman was slumped over a sign: "Pregnant and homeless. God bless you." As I pulled closer I saw she was sobbing.

I felt that old inadequacy, and when I dug deeper I saw that inadequacy was desperately trying to cover a chasm called "grief." So I let myself grieve, and as I did, I found myself pulling over to the lane close to her. All I had in the car was an apple left from my lunch. As I held it out, I heard myself talking to her like a human. Instead of showing her the pained face of someone who feels like a failure, for the first time in all my interactions with homeless people, I responded like a human talking to a human. The permission I'd taken earlier that day to say "I don't know" gave me a new confidence in my lack. I said something like, "I don't have much to give you and I wish I could do more. But I wanted to give you this and let you know someone cares."

Reflect

What makes you feel uncomfortable?

Emotions are sticky and confusing and unsatisfying. And when we're faced with them we think we have only two options: fix them or ignore them. But there's a third option: get used to the messiness and give them to God. Over and over and over again. This is the reason I walk and pray every morning, because I can't handle my life and emotions without it. It doesn't usually feel like being healed. Most days it feels like vomiting and asking God to clean it up. While my prayer is sometimes "Fix it" or "Heal it" or "Remove it," most days my prayer is just, "Take it! Take it! Take it!"

Reflect

Which emotions most knock you off your feet? How do you usually respond to that sudden vulnerability? How could it be an opportunity to lean on God?

5

I Need You!

How Vulnerable Pastors Pray

It's no new thing for pastors to pray. But how does a deep sense of our vulnerability affect our prayer life? Sometimes I pray because I should. But when I know how little I am up to the challenges of this work, prayer is a lifeline. How does prayer help us in this effort to admit our limits and trust his strength?

Around the time I became lead pastor, I walked and prayed the streets around the church, looking in the faces of people as they passed. They seem unmoved by my prayer, willing them to know God's love. I asked him to let me feel what he felt for this place, and he gave me the painful gift of his love for it. Whose crazy idea was it to pray, "Break my heart with the things that break yours"? Whatever tiny corner of God's heart he was revealing to me was more than my own little heart could bear. It ached like teenage angst, like the anguish of a lovelorn husband whose wife has turned to another. His wanting to be known became my prayer as I walked. It's strange to beg someone for something he wants even more than you do. His only response felt like a heavy sigh. So, together, we sighed.

As I walked, I wanted to leave a sign, to show this rational campus that mysterious things were happening here. So I brought chalk with me on my walks, and wherever I prayed I wrote, "I prayed here." It seemed like a harmless way to get our church engaged with the community, so I decided to make it a collaborative prayer experience. I made flyers, bought chalk in bulk and invited local ministries to join the monthlong walking and chalking "Prayer Point" initiative. I hoped it would get people talking, build community, start a prayer movement across the city. I wondered if it would even spark some media attention, imagined what I could say in an interview. Maybe it would become an opportunity to tell people how much God loved them.

The month of prayer walks was productive, but not in the way I had expected. We didn't get thousands involved in the church, we didn't get any press and the rain kept washing away any cumulative effect that our month of chalking might have had. Instead of starting a citywide movement, the most lasting effect it had was on my own heart. As I went around with my chalk and flyers, expecting this to be a winsome thing, I became limited by interpretation. Posting a flyer can feel like claiming turf. The flyers that weren't torn down seemed to dominate the landscape. So I just chalked "I prayed here" as I went. Then I wondered if writing "I prayed here" would be seen as a sign of domination. If I wrote it on someone's front steps or door, would it seem like I was claiming their home or business for a faith they didn't profess?

After passers-by asked, with indignation, "What are you praying for me?" I realized that prayer wasn't always welcome. To many, it was seen as staking territory. So I decided to write only on public property, which meant little more than the sidewalk. Now what had started as a playful experiment with colorful flyers and chalk became a month of kneeling on the sidewalk, aware of the awkwardness, pretending I didn't notice people watching me with bewilderment. Groups of students would gather around my words, look at each other, shrug and go on with their conversation. Didn't they know the Lord of all creation who had shaped them since inception, who knew their every fear and hope, was holding out in the bitter joy of the waiting? How could they just turn back to their decision between Thai or Indian for lunch?

If we're honest, we sometimes use prayer as a technology, a checklist for God to fix things. When all we feel is the sighing, the brokenness of ourselves and our world, prayer can become a way to just make it stop, to feel filled again, to imagine that God will make it all go away. And then we skip off to play until our next confrontation with the human condition. Instead, when we see all that is lacking in ourselves and our world, we need to go to prayer as a practice for embracing it, releasing emotion, crying for help. It's hard for prayers to fulfill that purpose when they remain polite and controlled. God wants to hear our need in all its wordless groaning, in all the color of feeling. This doesn't fix our brokenness but it lets us admit our lack. Prayer normalizes need and God can take it. And besides, asking for help is just what a small person does. Children know their need and are unashamed to ask.

There are many kinds of prayers: adoration, confession, thanksgiving, intercession, petition. But what if we have other things to say to God? Or we don't even know where to start? Or our negative feelings are directed toward him? When we feel forsaken by him, do we have to work through that on our own before we can talk to him about it? (What's the point of talking to someone who isn't there anyway?) What about when our hearts are too worn out to say anything? It's easy to just stop praying because we can't say the nice things we think prayer is supposed to say.

The Psalms give me hope that there is nothing too ugly or clumsy to say to God. In fact, in giving us permission to begin wherever we are, the Psalms show us a way back to the "pretty" prayers. Praying honest, raw prayers helps us move through anger, frustration and forsakenness and back to sincere thanksgiving and praise. Almost all major emotions are expressed in the Psalms—positive and negative feelings and even numbness. Because they're printed in clean text on crisp pages, we imagine the psalmist carefully editing them in his tidy office. But these are an outpouring of a raw human spirit, written in a rough hand.

Here are a few examples of some less-than-pretty prayers:

Feeling forgotten

How long, Lord? Will you forget me forever?
> How long will you hide your face from me?
How long must I wrestle with my thoughts
> and day after day have sorrow in my heart?
> How long will my enemy triumph over me? (Psalm 13:1-2)

Feeling forsaken

My God, my God, why have you forsaken me?
> Why are you so far from saving me,
> so far from my cries of anguish?
My God, I cry out by day, but you do not answer,
> by night, but I find no rest. (Psalm 22:1-2)

Overcome with shame

For I know my transgressions,
> and my sin is always before me.
Against you, you only, have I sinned
> and done what is evil in your sight. (Psalm 51:3-4)

Mourning

O God, the nations have invaded your inheritance;
> they have defiled your holy temple,
> they have reduced Jerusalem to rubble.
They have left the dead bodies of your servants
> as food for the birds of the sky,
> the flesh of your own people for the animals of the wild.
They have poured out blood like water
> all around Jerusalem,
> and there is no one to bury the dead. (Psalm 79:1-3)

Violence

Contend, Lord, with those who contend with me;
    fight against those who fight against me.
Take up shield and armor;
    arise and come to my aid.
Brandish spear and javelin
    against those who pursue me. (Psalm 35:1-3)

Before we go on, the violence of the imprecatory psalms deserves some extra attention here. They're not psalms we regularly read in church. This is partly because they need so much explanation, but it's also because, as the nation with the largest military in the history of humanity, we don't often find ourselves in the place the psalmist was when writing them. So they're not appropriate for the one in power to read. These psalms that call for God to overthrow someone else are not prayers of a king in his war room making a list of all his enemies and telling God to conquer more kingdoms and oppress more people. These are the prayers of one who is surrounded by accusers and attackers. There were times when David fled for his life, times when the city was surrounded by warring hordes. He felt abandoned, encircled by ravenous dogs. While we rarely have to fear for our lives, most of us have at some point felt surrounded by those who would undermine and accuse us. And here we have a model of how to pray even in those times.

We have sections of Scripture that are prescriptive and sections that are descriptive. These psalms are descriptions of how a real person felt. They aren't prescribing that we should feel that way but that, when we do, we should turn to God. Although these are violent words, they are a path to nonviolence because they call on God. Instead of taking his salvation into his own hands, the psalmist calls out to God. He says, "In whatever way those who seek my destruction are working against me, turn those efforts against them." This is a

defensive, not an offensive move: If they have dug a pit for me, may
they fall into it themselves.

These psalms give us permission to experience intense and negative
emotions and to bring them before God. It's hard at first to admit
these emotions to him, but he can handle them. Trust is built when
you beat your fists on his chest and he doesn't go anywhere. Comfort
is found in learning that there is no place we can go where God can't
be with us, even in our anger with him and, paradoxically, when we
feel he isn't there.

And in going there with God, we move through a process. In fact,
these psalms often range back and forth from questioning and com-
plaint to praise and statements of gratitude. So let's look at how these
same psalms end.

Psalm 13 goes from feeling forgotten to:

> But I trust in your unfailing love;
>> my heart rejoices in your salvation.
> I will sing the LORD's praise,
>> for he has been good to me. (Psalm 13:5-6)

Psalm 22 goes from feeling forsaken to:

> You who fear the LORD, praise him! . . .
> For he has not despised or scorned
>> the suffering of the afflicted one;
> he has not hidden his face from him
>> but has listened to his cry for help. (Psalm 22:23-24)

Psalm 51 goes from shame to:

> My sacrifice, O God, is a broken spirit;
>> a broken and contrite heart
>> you, God, will not despise. (Psalm 51:17)

Psalm 79 goes from mourning to:

Then we your people, the sheep of your pasture,
    will praise you forever;
from generation to generation
    we will proclaim your praise. (Psalm 79:13)

Psalm 35 goes from violence and calls for vindication to:

My tongue will proclaim your righteousness,
    your praises all day long. (Psalm 35:28)

In our efforts to pray "proper" prayers, we miss the opportunity to pray through a process that will help us to genuinely pray what we "should" pray. They don't feel like proper prayers, but my most common prayers are "Please let it all be true!" and "This feels too hard!" (which, out of faith, I chose to change from "This *is* too hard!") and "What are you going to do about this?" Praying *whatever* is on our heart, even if it's not pretty, will allow us to release it. Praying whatever is on our heart will remind us that God can handle our honesty. Knowing he has heard us feels like an answer in itself. And from there we learn to embrace our need for him.

While that prayer chalk project didn't become what I had expected, it took on a different shape. Toward the end of the month, while returning to my office from a prayer walk, I noticed the blankness of a large, purple wall in our church stairwell. So I wrote, "I prayed a purple prayer here" and dropped my chalk on the windowsill there. A day later I found that someone else had added a prayer. And a week later, there were three prayers. Now, months later, that entire stairwell has become our own impromptu purple wailing wall. A place to express exasperation, to ask questions, to say "help!" It's filled with prayers such as

"Save us!"

"We need you!"

"I'm tired!"

"Come, Lord, Jesus!"

"Thank you!"

"Show your power!"

"Release us from our darkness!"

"Heal me!"

"*Yes!*"

And there's even an "*Aaaargh!*"

Prayer Exercises

- When words are too much, or not enough, explore wordless prayers. Allow your heart to fill with whatever you feel, as mixed as the emotions may be. Without naming the feelings, just feel them, knowing that God knows them. They may make you want to yell or throw something or dance. Those can be prayers. While expressing the emotion may not alleviate it, at least it's a reminder that emotion is okay and we aren't expected to bear it alone.

- Visualization prayers allow us to imagine what we're asking for. Hold in your mind an image of a person or situation, like you and God are watching a slideshow together. As you "look at" each image, trust that the Father who looks at them with you knows them better than you do and knows your yearning for them as well. Paint a mental picture of how the situation seems to you and visualize an additional element as your prayer that God would act in the story. If you're sinking, add a lifeboat. If you're lost, create a light. When I'm feeling burdened, I imagine my arms filled with boulders (sometimes I name them—parenting, health, conflict), and one by one I imagine myself handing them to God, feeling the load lighten with each one. Miraculously, what felt like a boulder to me becomes a pebble to him, and as he drops each into his pocket, I can almost hear the tiny sound.

- Read Psalm 69 and note all the emotions the author expresses. If you are feeling those same emotions, find a guide in the author of the psalm. He is expert at finding a way from any emotion back to God.

- Take time to write your own psalm. What is on your heart to express to God? Whatever it is, he can handle it. It doesn't have to be profound, just sincere. (And it's okay even to say, "I don't know what to say.")

I had prayed that our neighborhood would know his love. As far as I know, our scrawling all over their streets for a month didn't contribute much to that effort. But I pray that, as members of the community use our building and climb those purple stairs, they will see a mess of prayers scrawled to the ceiling and watch how much a community of people knows the love of their Father and feels safe to call out to him for help.

Reflect

How has prayer been an effort to avoid vulnerability in your life? How can prayer grow from vulnerability?

6

Letting the Bible Read Us

How Vulnerable Pastors Read the Bible

We do not read [Scripture] in order to find out how to get God into our lives. . . . No. We open this book and find that page after page it takes us off guard, surprises us and draws us into its reality, pulls us into participation with God on his terms. . . . Reading is an immense gift, but only if the words are assimilated, taken into the soul—eaten, chewed, gnawed, received in unhurried delight.

EUGENE PETERSON, *EAT THIS BOOK: A CONVERSATION IN THE ART OF SPIRITUAL READING*

For most of us, the Bible is so familiar it's become part of the furniture, an object to tidy from the table when it's time for dinner and to bring out when it's time to work. But perhaps it's not an object in our world. Perhaps we're creatures in its. What would it mean to make the vulnerable choice to open ourselves as we open it, to let it work on us as we work from it?

I have to be honest: I've often wished for a new revelation. It seems about time for God to provide the next chapter of Scripture. It takes more energy than I have most weeks to dig through culture, language and history to unearth some kernel of truth from Scripture and to know enough about our own time to find a place to plant it. I'm not asking for new ideas. It would just be nice to have a word directly from God with less sheep and wheat and girding of loins and more pets and supermarkets and traffic jams.

> We pastors are like starving chefs, working diligently to prepare the best meals we can for others while our own souls run the risk of withering away. Why? Because we too rarely approach the table simply to eat, to enjoy, to feast on what God has prepared for us. We rarely come to Scripture with our own hearts in mind.
>
> Bob Hyatt[1]

When I've expressed this frustration to God, I've sensed his answer to be, *You're the new revelation.* Not me personally. And not in the sense that we're receiving new information. But you and I are the new revelation as we apply ancient Scripture to our twenty-first-century lives. This is how his living, active Word is incarnate in us. As we wrestle with living Scripture today, new truth will be revealed. His Word will be embodied in us. As much as it would be easier to have a fresh word, we don't need another testament. We've got the truth. It just wants to be integrated into real human hearts, minds, homes and cities.

It would be easy to tuck ourselves away in a cave, safe from the world, and think only about Scripture. On the other hand, it would also be easy to immerse ourselves in the next trend, free to be of the moment. But it's our task to discover how truth in the Bible and in the world fit together. The world doesn't need another system or more easy answers. It needs to see how this Word has smashed and rebuilt us. And how we're learning to live it in a place of pets, supermarkets and traffic jams.

When we step into ministry, we think we're giving our time and our gifts. And God is more than happy to take those. But then he says, "And I'll take everything else too, thank you very much." He wants our whole stories, including our weaknesses. He sees how our whole lives can be a testing ground for lessons he wants to teach others through us. And so as we engage honestly with Scripture, allowing it to be living and active in our twenty-first-century lives, we're able to reveal it in fresh ways in this culture. But as you know, it's a tiring and scary prospect to hand over everything we have and everything we are to be shaped and used. What does it mean to allow Scripture to read us? What does that mean for how we teach it?

Reflect

Do you experience a longing for Scripture to be easier to understand, apply and teach? How do you respond to it? How do you respond to your own heart and life being part of the process?

A HERMENEUTIC OF *HĒSYCHIA*

As a younger woman in Bible college, I found myself caught between the Bible and a hard place. On the one hand, I was often told what I, as a woman, couldn't do because the God of the Bible had said so. On the other hand, the God in my heart was telling me about all the things he wanted me to do. When my male classmates had theoretical discussions about gender roles, I could join the discussions for only so long because I knew "women" meant me. My culture had taught me to respond with "It's my right!" and "It's my turn!" I began to feel that the system was unredeemable and demanded an aggressive response.

I had female friends who felt a strong call to ministry but who set it aside because they didn't want to mess with questions about Scripture (or deal with people who opposed their sense of call). And I had other friends who disagreed so strongly with Christian restrictions on gender roles that they walked away from their faith entirely. I wasn't comfortable with either choice. But I also wasn't resolved in how the God in my life and the God in Scripture came together.

And then I came across a lesson in the least likely place: the disquieting 1 Timothy 2:11-12 passage. A Greek word study pointed out that the word translated "quiet" or "silent" (*hēsychia*) is not simply auditory silence but implies an element of inner peace.[2] In fact, the same root word is used earlier in the chapter, and that section is usually translated "that we may live peaceful and quiet lives" (1 Timothy 2:2). What kind of cruel irony had embedded this peace directive in the very source of my discontent? While I didn't yet fully understand the implications of this passage on my call to ministry, I knew one thing: I did not have a tranquil heart. I was doing what my culture had taught me to do: fight for my rights. And although I didn't yet know what leadership should look like for women, I came to see that no Christian leadership can grow from the demanding of rights.

And so with some gritting of teeth, and although I didn't yet have a resolution to my questions (and wouldn't for years to come), I decided that whatever the answer was, it had to come from a place of peace. Peace that God is One, that the God who is in Scripture is the same God who is calling me to ministry. Peace that he would bring clarity from the mess and healing for my angst. For many years I sat in the tension between what I felt and what Scripture seemed to say, waiting on the God who is One, asking him to teach me *hēsychia*. While there are many things I'm not proud of in my past, I'm proud of the day my twenty-something self chose that uncomfortable place. The pain of not knowing made me long for quick answers, but I knew that a rushed solution was not a good solution. It was a painful five years of reading, prayer, conversations, journaling and tears.

It troubles me that our efforts to understand God often result in demeanors that deny him—anxiety, domination, manipulation, divisiveness. Our theology often becomes about human power, a loss of mystery and peace. When we can embrace a hermeneutic of *hēsychia*, we are able to trust that things that seem to conflict can be resolved, whether the conflict arises from apparent inconsistencies within Scripture, disagreements among believers, or ways that Scripture conflicts with our own hearts or our culture. Embracing mystery in our study of Scripture will teach us his deeper mysteries. Having peace in our study of Scripture will help us find the God of peace. Releasing control will help us experience his power.

After those five years of wrestling came many new issues to wrestle with and many more temptations to find quick answers. We think we are working toward answers, but all along God is working on us. To see how the God in our hearts, in our world and in Scripture is One, it will take a change of our hearts.

> The knowledge-as-information approach is about power. . . . The point of knowledge is to eliminate wonder and mystery. It's to put humans in control of the world. . . . Is a vision of life, of reality, as finally about love and shalom something that we can believe? Or are we compelled to think that ultimately reality is personless, meaningless, chaotic, warring? The latter is well-suited to seeking power and domination. For if that is all there is, it doesn't matter how we treat it. In the face of meaninglessness, domination is a better strategy.
> **Esther Lightcap Meek**[3]

Reflect

How is it hard for you to trust that God in Scripture, culture and life is One? What would it look like to embrace a hermeneutic of *hēsychia*?

DISSECTION OR FIELD RESEARCH?

Hebrews 4:7-13 says,

> God again set a certain day, calling it "Today." This he did when a long time later he spoke through David, as in the passage already quoted:

"Today, if you hear his voice,
> do not harden your hearts."

For if Joshua had given them rest, God would not have spoken later about another day. There remains, then, a Sabbath-rest for the people of God; for anyone who enters God's rest also rests from their works, just as God did from his. Let us, therefore, make every effort to enter that rest, so that no one will perish by following their example of disobedience.

For the Word of God is alive and active. Sharper than any double-edged sword, it penetrates even to dividing soul and spirit, joints and marrow; it judges the thoughts and attitudes of the heart. Nothing in all creation is hidden from God's sight. Everything is uncovered and laid bare before the eyes of him to whom we must give account.

As you read those words, did you feel the movement of something living and active? Did you feel your soul and spirit divided, your thoughts and attitudes judged? Probably not. Just as I didn't notice anything significant happening as I copied and pasted them into my manuscript. So what does that say about the Word of God? Why is it not always powerful?

Sometimes we're just tired or distracted. But often it's because we've brought our own unstated expectations to the Bible. We all do it—form Scripture to our own agendas. We use it as a weapon to cut down arguments, and while Scripture is undoubtedly powerful, it is God's power, not ours. We use it as a rule book, and of course it contains guidelines for life but not directives to force on every decision. We try it out as a textbook, but often it's not trying to answer the questions we bring to it. Or we make it our pet. While it can certainly be comforting and can "perform," it's not tame or in our control. On the other hand, we are tempted to make it an idol, and while it is from God, it's not God. We bring many agendas to God's Word that get in the way of its power.

So, what *is* this Word of God? In this passage from Hebrews, it's a story of a God waiting for human hearts to be willing to receive what he longs to give them. Even in this short, seven-verse passage there's a reference to creation, to Joshua, to David's time and to the first-century context. So in this one brief section of Scripture, we see God's movement throughout all of human history, and here we are reading it thousands of years later. This living, active Word of God has been working throughout the story of humanity. And it continues to long for human hearts to rest long enough to receive his work.

But those of us in ministry come to this book as professionals to do *our* work. We're expected to have something to show for our efforts. People who study living and active things often go out and capture those living, active things and bring them into a laboratory. They organize them in neat little jars. To understand, they kill that living, active thing. We're all guilty of it. We approach Scripture like lab technicians, dissecting God's Word so that we can understand and manage it. Are our skills and training tools to help us engage honestly with the Word or technologies to dominate it?

Another way to study living, active things is to step into their natural habitat, to do field research. Which is much more scary than lab work. Field researchers humbly wait until the wild thing shows itself. They live in the thing's natural habitat, waiting for days, maybe weeks, for a glimpse of what they study. When it chooses to show itself, the chase is on! It's humbling and sometimes frightening to pursue a living, active thing.

If we are going to study something living and active, will we kill it in the process or are we up for an adventure? Will we set aside our formaldehyde and scalpels long enough to venture into the wide space where it lives and patiently learn its habits? Even if it means we are transformed by the chase? When we're at our desks preparing our sermons and something snags our hearts, can we set aside our work long enough to be worked upon? Can we trust that the teaching of our congregations is not primarily our work but God's work, which he wants to begin with us? Will we trust that there is time for us to learn and still find a meaningful message by Sunday? Will we trust that our willingness to be transformed may make the Word more meaningful, even if we're still learning when we teach?

Still, this Hebrews text does talk about something that sounds like dissection. And here's where the passage becomes surreal, like one of those nightmares where one thing strangely becomes something else—you're in your house but at some point it turns into your high school as well. We've set aside our scalpels, stepped into the habitat of this living thing, watched its ways and breathlessly tried to keep up with it. We want to let it live so we can understand it more and more, even if it means being exhausted by the chase.

But suddenly there's a knife! Where did it come from? We don't want to do dissection here. We want to keep the Word alive! But the Word is not the thing under the knife; *we* are. We're on the table, hearts still pounding from the chase, awaiting our fate. How did we get here?

Suddenly we realize that what we thought was a laboratory table is actually an operating table. We are not in the hands of a lab technician but a surgeon. And he is not carving up a dead thing; he is doing surgery to heal a living thing.

This living, active thing is sharper than any double-edged sword, penetrating to divide soul and spirit, joints and marrow, judging the thoughts and attitudes of our hearts. Suddenly this living and active thing is doing surgery on us, inviting us to rest in a place where we are naked and laid bare, where we allow it to make difficult cuts, to judge the thoughts and intentions of our hearts. We long to experience the power of God's Word, but really we'd rather wield that power, not submit to it. It's excruciating to expose ourselves in this way—allowing God to do the work, trusting that he is a good surgeon, that his incisions work only to remove whatever drains our life. Are we willing to allow God's Word to do that kind of work on our hearts? Are we willing to rest on that operating table, naked and laid bare?

We don't relish the thought of surgery. When we sense it coming, we tend to harden our hearts. We know it will feel like death and we don't trust that there's resurrection behind it. And so we stay safe, bringing our own agendas, doing our work on the Word instead of entering into rest so *it* can work.

I write about this with some trepidation, remembering the times I've shakily chosen to lay myself on that operating table when everything inside told me to run. One day in particular comes to mind—a day that felt like death and absolute nakedness. While at the time it didn't feel like a good day, I now know it was. No one can live forever in surgery. But at the same time, we live because of days like this one.

Are We There Yet?

The story begins in 1989 in Brisbane, Australia. Jamie and I were looking at places to go to Bible college, and since our own denomination was going through some upheaval at the time, we had difficulty finding a place to study in Australia. At the same time we met some people from Cincinnati who offered Jamie a scholarship. So we decided to come to the United States to study. Since we had seen many Australians leave Australia for Bible college, we decided to go overseas to study and then come back to Australia. It seemed very noble—a calling from God even.

So three months out of high school I married Jamie, and three months later we left for Cincinnati. We studied there for six years then moved to England for his doctorate. The plan was to study for a total of ten years, then return to Australia to teach. And that all worked well until around the ten-year mark. As Jamie was finishing up his PhD, we looked for opportunities back in Australia. But around that time, our denomination's Bible college in our hometown, where we had hoped to one day work, closed its doors. Soon after, Jamie was invited to apply to teach back in Cincinnati where we had studied earlier. It wasn't what we had expected, but we had the "When God closes a door, he opens a window" approach. We thought, *We're still trusting the God who will take us home. He's been with us for ten years. Maybe he's giving us this opportunity to get some experience first.* So in 1998 we came to Cincinnati for two years. I'm writing this sixteen years later, looking out my window at that Bible college where we were going to spend two years.

Because we trusted in the God who would take us home, we applied for anything we could find that would take us back to Australia. It happened about every six months. If you've ever been through the process of applying for positions, you know it's a roller coaster ride. That's even more the case with international job applications, which can string themselves out over months of phone calls and interviews. You start to look at houses and schools and your heart packs its suitcases. But with an international application, there's a lot at stake for the employer, and often the selection came down to us and one other person who was local. It always went to the local person, the one who knew the right people and could interview in person.

Then would come the "Thanks but no thanks" letter and we'd come crashing down. Every six months. Whatever roots we'd pulled up we had to set back down. Every six months. For years we lived in that in-between place. Our daughter, Zoë, who has journaled since she could hold a pencil, would turn to the back page of each new journal and write, "Zoë of the future, are you in Australia yet?" There were many journals like that. We said *"when* we go," not "if." We trusted in the God who would take us home. Zoë is a teenager now. Sixteen years of saying "when" is exhausting.

Eventually I couldn't distinguish anymore between my sense of calling to work in Australia and my deep desire to have Christmas with my family. During this time it seemed like my entire extended family was in a coma, not quite dead but out of reach. Every six months, each job application process was like getting a call from the hospital saying, "We think they're waking up! Come now!" We'd grab our stuff and run out the door, only to find on arrival at the hospital the disappointed faces and apologies. "Sorry. False alarm." Our whole life was lived on that roller coaster. I can't even remember how many times I cried about it.

About two years ago, a perfect opportunity to minister in Australia dropped into our laps, ours for the taking. But at the same time we were busy with our ministries here. Not only was it not a good time to make a major change, it wasn't a good time to even talk about a major change. So for several months we prayed. And argued. After one argument over this job opportunity, Jamie left for work. As he did, I felt God pressing on my shoulders with the words, *You have to let it go.* I didn't have to decide to go or not to go, but to loosen my grip, to give it to him. If a heart can yell, mine yelled that day, asking, "Do you want me to trust in the God who gave me the promise or the God who is asking me to kill the promise?"

You can imagine which story from Scripture came to mind here. There are times when you should read the Bible and there are other times when you must. As much as I hated the story of Abraham's call to sacrifice Isaac, I had to read it. I felt called by God to sacrifice something I thought was *from* God. That day I came to understand the story in a deeper way, the way tears and marrow understand.

To help me explore how this ancient story was being pressed into my own beating heart, I made a collage, a domesticated version of the altar Abraham made. On a little paper fireplace I glued tiny pieces of kindling, and on the kindling I laid words like *home* and *future* and *happiness*. To an onlooker it may have seemed I was doing a little scrapbooking. But in my heart, with each scrap of paper I glued I was laying down my hopes. Over the kindling I pasted a mantelpiece, and on it a lit candle. On the wall I hung crossed swords. Abraham had the fire and the knife; he had what it took to make a sacrifice. I may have had shaking hands, but I wanted to show I meant it. I was laying these things down. *I don't know where you're leading, Father, but I'm sick of this.*

Above the mantelpiece I was sure to add a ram—a tiny framed print of a sheep, offering itself as an option to the flame and the sword.

There's always the ram, Lord. Don't forget the ram! I know how the Genesis story goes. So it's fine with me if you go with the ram.

It breaks my heart even remember that day. Recently when I preached from that passage of Scripture, I found myself overwhelmed with anxious tears as I read it aloud, like a frightened child being dragged back to a dark place. I did not want to revisit it. I still felt the pain of having to give up something I had grasped so tightly for so long.

But now when I look back on that day I have a clearer sense of what God was doing. He was asking me, *Do you trust in the God who will take you home? Or do you just trust?* I wonder if God was asking Abraham, *Do you trust in the God who will give you a child? Or do you just trust?* It felt like surgery to carve off that little phrase. Because for a long time I had trusted in the God who would take me home. And he hadn't taken me home. What did that mean? That day I chose to say, *Even if you never take me home, even if I lose everything, I just trust.*

What I think I actually sacrificed that day was my two-dimensional cardboard cutout of God. And I have never been more free. I still can't tell you why I'm not in Australia. But I don't feel called to any one place; I feel called to the church. And the church is everywhere. That's all I have—to serve the church wherever I am. So we had a "We're not going away" party. To just be where we were. Maybe one day God will take us somewhere else. And then we'll be there. But my ability to be available for my current role, which I love, came about because of that day.

Experiences like that teach me how I have often approached Scripture like a scientist with a scalpel—controlling, dissecting, labeling. I'm learning that to engage with the Word is to engage with far more than a book. After a day like that, I'm learning with trepidation to trust Scripture to be the living, active Word of God, dividing soul from spirit, joints from marrow, judging

Today, if you hear his voice, do not harden your hearts.
Hebrews 4:7

the thoughts and intentions of my heart. I am naked and laid bare to the eyes of the Great Surgeon. One whose incisions will sting as they slice out malignant growth but will leave me more whole and healthy. I choose to enter into his rest, setting aside my work of dissection to be the one worked upon.

Each surgery feels like a little death and a lot of rebirth. To truly embrace that kind of transformative power, we have to trust that the surgeon is good and that the rest he's calling us to is good. We have to trust that if we allow our hearts to be open, ourselves to be naked and laid bare, that there is healing ahead. The world doesn't need to see nicely labeled dead ideas in jars. It needs to see that, although our stitches still smart, there's resurrection in our eyes.

Reflect

How do you try to control Scripture? How is God calling you to rest from your work so that he can do his work?

Exercises to Engage Scripture as Whole Beings

Both ministry education and personal Bible study often look like sitting alone, reading and writing. Those are certainly a part of our study, but if they're the only way we approach the text, we engage Scripture with just one part of ourselves—the rational, professional part. And that's not enough. This is not a question of emotional versus intellectual engagement or practical versus conceptual engagement but partial versus whole-self engagement. In addition to traditional approaches to studying Scripture, try a few approaches that engage new parts of yourself:

- Embrace the learning embedded in all aspects of our work. Colossians 3:16 says, "Let the message of Christ dwell among you richly as you teach and admonish one another with all wisdom through psalms, hymns, and songs from the Spirit, singing to God with gratitude in your hearts." How can we learn from Scripture even while engaging in community and worshiping together?
- Marinate in Bible passages. Memorize short sections to ruminate on in the unfilled spaces of your days so that the passage can be in conversation with your life.
- Don't expect all learning to happen while you're in front of a book or a screen. Build in unstructured space for dreaming to reflect on what you've read. Tasks like mowing, sweeping and working out set up a comforting rhythm that create a framework for creative, reflective thought.
- Write out a passage by hand. (Try it with the hand you don't usually use!)
- Listen to audio recordings of Scripture or read aloud. Try several translations.[4]
- Journal your own personal collisions with Scripture, not only the well-worded lessons but also the questions and clues you find along the way. Collect magazine articles, quotes, photos, sketches, songs—whatever seems meaningful, even if you're not sure why. That way the journal becomes a tool for the process instead of just a place to record end products.
- Write out a personal brainstorming session of all the things (a movie, a person, a memory?) that come to mind when you're reading a passage. They don't have to make sense and you don't have to even explain why this passage brings them to mind.
- Reflect on your history with a passage, things you've learned from it previously, ways it makes you uncomfortable.

- Ask what wasn't included in this telling of the story. Why did the author choose to include what is included? What information did the author choose not to include?
- In whatever way you're creative (writing, cooking, parenting, gardening, fixing), find a way to express this passage in that medium.
- Do *lectio divina* with a passage. For me, that means reading it slowly several times with silence between to reflect on a different question after each reading, often:
  1. What is a word or phrase that is meaningful from the passage (without explaining why)?
  2. How do you see Christ in the passage?
  3. How do you feel called to respond?

  This can be done alone but can be even better with a group. Hearing from others helps you get a multifaceted reading of the text.[5]

- Set aside reference materials and read the passage according to its genre. If it's poetry, let it be poetic. If it's narrative, let it be a story worth repeating. Let it stand on its own two feet.
- Call a friend and ask what this passage means to him or her. Bring the passage to a Bible study group to toss it around with others.
- Search online and read what others have said about the passage, even if you disagree with them. Search for music, art or stained glass windows that this passage has inspired.
- Give yourself permission to dig deep with a small section of Scripture. Covering a lot of the Bible is not as important as living a small section of it one piece at a time.
- How does your physical setting influence your reading of the passage? Would reading in your kids' treehouse be different from on the bus? Allow it to interact with new places and you may see it in new ways.
- Consider how you choose passages for upcoming sermons and Bible studies. Is it based on what God is teaching you at the moment or a great idea you once had? Do you choose a passage because you know a lot about it or because you want to stretch yourself? Is it based on what your congregation and community need? Is there a way that what you're learning and what God is doing in your community are connected? How can they learn from what he's teaching you and how can you learn from what he's doing in them?

PART TWO

BEING TRUE
TO OURSELVES

Vulnerability Behind the Scenes

7

Learning to Like the Mess

How Vulnerable Pastors Create Culture

When I was a kid, if you'd asked what kind of family culture I wanted to make for my own kids one day, I would have looked up from some art project and said, without hesitation, "A creative one!" While I was expecting my first child I was already gathering art supplies, dreaming of the projects we would do together. So it was with some surprise that I soon discovered an even stronger (but as-yet-unnamed) desire—one for order.

As much as I loved the idea of raising kids in a creative home culture, my deeper compulsion for neatness had me cringing at spilled paint and constantly picking up behind a child in inventor mode. If my son wanted to build a LEGO house with a book for the roof, when playtime was over, the LEGO bricks had to be back with the LEGO bricks, the book back with the books. How had a creative, messy kid grown up to become so controlling?

When this disturbing realization and its ramifications came to me, I knew I had a choice to make—creativity and obsessive tidiness rarely coexist. If I really wanted to nurture a creative home culture, I had to choose the discomfort, get over some baggage and make conscious choices instead of gut reactions.

We don't always live out what we claim to value. When we as

leaders describe our staff or church culture, we may find that our description reflects our ideals more than reality. How would our culture be described by those who live in it (or who've left it)? We may say our culture is honest, but when someone disagrees with us, does our facial expression shut her down? We may say our culture welcomes ideas, but when they are offered, do we switch into critic mode? We may think we're human-friendly, but when someone calls in sick, does our response reveal the weight of the work he won't get done? Creating culture is more than *saying* what our culture is; it's *being* it, over and over until it becomes who we truly are. This means that one of the best ways we as leaders can nurture and live out a healthy human culture is to know and face our own "junk." It may mean we have to choose the discomfort, get over some baggage and make conscious choices instead of gut reactions.

> [The distinguishing factor between organizations that disintegrate and those that flourish is] the presence of *a well-differentiated leader....* I mean someone who has clarity about his or her own life goals, and, therefore, someone who is less likely to become lost in the anxious emotional processes swirling about. I mean someone who can be separate while still remaining connected, and therefore can maintain a modifying, non-anxious, and sometimes challenging presence. I mean someone who can manage his or her own reactivity to the automatic reactivity of others, and therefore be able to take stands at the risk of displeasing.
>
> **Edwin H. Friedman**[1]

While the culture we're shaping at my church is showing itself to be healthy, it didn't begin with a well-defined, detached definition of what church culture should be. Whatever part I've played in culture shaping began from my knowledge of my limitations, trusting that God knows his church does what it does through and for humans and so needs to account for human limitation. Let's take some time to explore some of the key features of a healthy and vulnerable ministry culture.

HUMAN

As we flipped through her wedding photos, a friend commented on the "human scale" of the chapel. Her architect husband explained how the proportions of the human body are considered when designing spaces. Whether or not we name it, we feel small in cavernous spaces and designers of great halls use that effect to communicate grandeur and awe. On the other hand, when there is a more natural ratio of our body to the space it's in, we feel less awed by the space and more welcomed into it. It's a fascinating concept for the design of buildings and cities but also for the design of ministries.[2]

Often we begin ministry with a sense of something huge—an immense task, a great need, a vision of God's grandeur, an overwhelming sense of call—then we shape a ministry program to respond to that vast challenge. Out of a pure sense of survival, I tried starting the other way. What if we began with our human limitations and shaped a ministry from that? Like a child pouring pennies on a candy store counter, asking, "How much candy can I get with that?" we can look at the time, gifts, energy and ideas we have and ask, "How much church can we get with that?"

I've moved internationally three times for my husband's studies and work. At times I wondered what that would mean for my calling. But if it was right for Jamie to do these things (and I believed it was), and it was right for me to be with him (and I believed it was), then my support of Jamie's gifts and passions was not going to keep God from using mine. Another chance to learn the peace, to embrace the hermeneutic of *hēsychia*. This *hēsychia* prepared me for the possibility when I stepped into my current ministry role that God was also able to work around the fact that I'm a human being. If it's right for me to be here (and I believe it is) and it's all right for me to be limited (and I believe it is), I have to trust that there's a way to do this job without it destroying me. If he gave the church to humans, he must have a way for humans to do church.

Our humanity means we need each other, so church needs to be collaborative, equipping and transparent. The ways we grow together will be messy, so our culture needs to be experimental, flexible and comfortable with process.[3] Trusting that God can work even in our human messiness makes us more playful, less afraid of mistakes. We take ourselves less seriously, not because we take our work lightly, but because it's not all up to us. Opening our minds to the possibility that God can work with human limitation means we have no choice but to embrace mystery. So our entire culture grows from an acknowledgment of our human limitations and brings us to a new comfort with our limited understanding of an unlimited God. It's a culture that leaves room for him. And he can work with that.

Reflect

How do you usually experience your own limitations? On the other hand, what time or gifts are in your hand? How much church could you get with that?

COLLABORATIVE AND EQUIPPING

I confess that in parenting I don't naturally invite the kids into cooking and cleaning. Including them means the work will be slower, messier and will no longer taste or look quite the way I would have it. That same instinct shows itself in my ministry. And when it does, it means that I do all the work myself (and resent it). Plus, it has only my "flavor" and no one else learns to do anything. Not good for me, for the work or for them.

When I've discovered this about myself, I've gone to the opposite extreme of dropping others in the deep end. It's not my job anymore— now it's yours. Good luck with that! It's easy to do it myself; it's easy to hand it wholesale over to someone else. What is harder than either is the choice that is most healthy: to equip someone else to do it. And so any conversation about collaboration also needs to be about equipping.

My instinct, when I'm overwhelmed by the amount or complexity of work before me, is to hyperengage. I'm learning instead to see the feeling of being overwhelmed as a signal to collaborate. When I collaborate, I unpack what my process would have been if I'd done the work: the questions, concerns, resources. Instead of wrestling with them myself, I pass them on for someone else to wrestle with. So currently I have two families leading a conversation with the parents in the church about the future of family ministry, a barista researching third place ministries, and a small group exploring what sabbath looks like on a community level. In each place I ask where they need more of me and where they need less.

My job is not to have all the answers; neither is it to step entirely out of the way. My job is to shape the process and invite people into it, always keeping the bigger picture of our mission at the center of it all. If we were making soup, it would be my job to describe the kind of soup we're making and invite each person to bring his or her own ingredient. I'm open to creative options ("Nutmeg, you say? It's unusual, but maybe . . . "). But I need to remind them we're making soup here, not pudding or papier-mâché—so chocolate chips or glue are best kept for other projects. This equipping means digging into what is instinctive to me when I'm running the show, unearthing my motivations and concerns and putting those into words for others. And as I learn to do all this, not only do I feel weight lifted from my own shoulders; I see how beautifully others bear it, how what gave me stress gives them joy. Whatever we create together no longer takes on just my single flavor but now has a satisfying complexity of many flavors.

For this reason I ask all my staff to lead the doxology at the end of our service—even those who can't sing. It's one of the best metaphors of ministry there is. All you have to do is pick a note and sing it, regardless of your own fears of whether it's a good note. And so far, the congregation has never yet left me hanging. I start with "Praise . . ." and by the time we get to "God from whom all blessings flow," there's a swell of a hundred voices. One line into the song, we're already beginning to feel we're experiencing something together. And it didn't take a rehearsal or big band or any budget or even much talent on my part. All it took to start was one little (sometimes shaky) voice.

As I sing, I know I get a goofy grin on my face as the voices wash over me. At first I smile just because they sound so beautiful. But then my smile broadens because it's my weekly reminder that we're doing ministry together, that God can take my feeble squeak and create a heavenly choir. As I sing, I'm reminded of whatever I've tried to do for him that week and I know that he can take one tired conversation and create a deep relationship; he can take one flat sermon and create encouragement in the heart of a listener. My work never seems fresh or creative or finished enough, but God is able to make it enough. And so one way I equip my leaders is to remind them it's their job to equip others. We're not soloists; we're choirmasters. It's not our job to do the work but to give the direction: to pick the note, choose when to start and wait for the community to shape the fullness of the song.

> Ship your grain across the sea;
>
> after many days you may receive a return. (Ecclesiastes 11:1)

Reflect

How are you tempted to do it all yourself? How are you tempted to drop it all on others? How are you replicating yourself? What would it look like to commission the church community to watch for needs and listen to God?

TRANSPARENT

One morning I went to the church early to pray about an early morning argument before getting on with the day's work. When I stepped into the office, I was surprised to find Anthony, one of my associate pastors, also there early. I said a quick "hi," dropped my stuff and left for the bathroom with eyedrops, makeup and tissues in hand. But as soon as I locked the door behind me, I knew that a little mascara would not hide my state of mind. So against my instincts of self-preservation, I marched back in there and admitted my state to my coworker. I had no idea where it would lead, only that I couldn't pretend. And it became much more than an opportunity for me to be authentic for my own sake. He saw that leaders don't always have perfect families, asked how he could pray for me and offered his ideas for a decision my morning hadn't allowed me to make. It wasn't the illusion of control and organization that I had hoped to create by coming in early that day, but it became something even better.

Experiences like this with staff have given me the courage to step into transparency with the congregation. When I feel the pressure to have it all together, to fully understand the Bible, to have all the answers, it's tempting to spend a lot of time in the bathroom, preparing myself to emerge with a fake smile and a ready-made answer. But I've decided that, even if it's only for the sake of my own soul and sanity, I have to be myself. It's shown me God's comfort with my humanity as he uses my honesty to encourage others that he's comfortable with their humanity. Whether it's in staff meetings or sermons, small groups or budget meetings, the humans we lead need to see it's normal to wrestle, have doubts, feel numb. It's freeing for them to know the pastor feels that way—and keeps following God. Our example becomes not ourselves but our need for him.

I'm still learning when and with whom and how deeply to share my true self. I have a subconscious sliding scale that takes into consideration factors about the person or people in question: their age, spiritual maturity, position in the church, relationship to me, relationship to others involved in my problem. I ask myself, *Are you holding back because*

you don't want to burden them? Or are you holding back to protect yourself?
And, *Are you sharing to bring attention to yourself or to God?*

It helps to check where I am in my own process. If I have no words
at all, I know God is the only one who can handle it. If I need to vent
and say things I don't really mean, I keep that for my husband or a
trusted counselor or peer outside of the church. If I'm at the stage
where I can be honest about the problem but still end with a sincere,
"But I know God is good" or "Somehow it will be okay," then I know
I'm ready to share it with church leaders or senior staff. If I've processed
it enough that I can sum up my struggle in a sentence or two (without
necessarily having resolution), I know I'm ready to share it with younger
church members. One thing I know for sure: we won't learn to be
comfortable with healthy transparency by thinking about it. We have
to step into it, which means giving ourselves grace and asking for grace
for the times we don't get it right. In the end, the best transparency will
grow from sharing what builds up others—no more, no less.

Reflect

Think back to times you've under- and overshared. What made them
appropriate or inappropriate? Were you motivated by your own interests or the interests of others? What makes the difference between
good and bad transparency?

EXPERIMENTAL

I'm a perfectionist, but not a very good one.

This became apparent when I signed up for worship band. I'd been
in bands before. I knew the drill—get the sheet music, take it home
and practice until it was perfect. But this band leader's bluegrass background meant he thought it was perfectly reasonable to hand a flute
player a chord chart and say, "Just play what you feel."

For years in orchestra I'd been told, "Stop tapping your toes!" Feeling wasn't even mentioned.

So I took home those chord charts and carefully made notations of every trill so that my "improvisations" would seem seamless. But soon I started straying from my notes. The music began coming from a new place until one Sunday morning I found myself gazing at the rafters and playing with all my heart. Frantically I searched for my place on the page, wondering how long I'd been floating away from the safety of the precious notes on my music stand. I froze in fear, realizing I had no idea what note was next. So of course the next note was wrong, but that day I learned a new kind of music, no longer performing what had been written by someone else but expressing something from inside myself.

In the past, controlling every note had made my performances consistently adequate. Now improvising meant risking catastrophe for the sake of making something new. I soon found that this new playfulness trickled into other areas of my life. I hadn't made art in years because my detailed, careful work was never good enough. The blank page had taunted me.

Will it be good? If not, why bother even starting?

Whenever the time had come to make art, I had fearfully taken a pencil with a fine point (paint was much too messy) and made something small and afraid. And somehow both it and I felt less for its creation. But now, with my newfound risky flute skills, I set aside my pointed pencils, picked up a fat house-painting brush and got slap-happy with it. Not only did my heart learn to paint, my paintings were better than ever before.

At every turn in ministry we are presented with blank canvases. Whether it's a new program, idea, role or ministry direction, we're tempted to stop in our tracks and ask, *Will it be good? If not, why bother even starting?* Do we wait until we have every question ironed out before we begin? Or are we willing to start with what we have?

> No longer need Christian communities anxiously glance over their shoulder, lest they make a terrible mistake that betrays their performance of the script. Instead they can trust the practices and patterns of their common life and have confidence that God joins in their faithful improvisation.
>
> **Sam Wells**[4]

These improvisation lessons found new application when I began to be considered for the lead pastor role. As I rehearsed my résumé and a feeble five-year plan, my heart, after worshiping with this community for years, looked on all my posturing and simply thought, *I just love this place.* A reassurance, which I believe was from above, replied, *Go with that.* So I did.

And I do. There are still plans to be made, meetings to be led, budgets to be balanced and sermons to be written. But I'm learning not to let their blankness taunt. That question *Will it be good? If not, why bother even starting?* turns me inward, makes me focus on what others think of me, makes my congregation the enemy to protect myself from, the audience to perform for. How can that possibly be a place of generosity or service? Instead I'm learning to look at any blankness before me—any unwritten sermon, any unanswered question, any unresolved problem, any unknowable or uncontrollable thing—and turn inward just long enough to see what I have there to share. It may be as simple and unimpressive as love or hope or faith. It feels childish and vulnerable and unprofessional. But it's how Jesus led. He invited people into his joy, and we can too.[5]

Reflect

What feels to you like a blankness that taunts? How could you start somewhere even if you don't know what shape it might take? What seemingly small thing do you have to share?

COMFORTABLE WITH PROCESS

Process is probably a word I say too much. One clue that's true: my entire

American congregation has started saying it with my Australian accent: "PRO-cess." I don't talk about it endlessly because I naturally love it (or tension or mess, for that matter). It's because I've wrestled with process and process has won. Process gets its way and I don't. I'd much rather talk about control and order. They offer the possibility that before I start anything I can know exactly where it will lead me. They offer simple answers, clarity. The problem is, they're illusions. We can fight it or ignore it but process will always find us.

> The modern world lays such emphasis on the work product and stresses productivity so relentlessly that process is only seen as a means to this end.... Process is ... one of those words we cannot slight when we speak of art—or growth, for that matter. The healing properties of the experience are bound into the process.
> **Joan M. Erikson**[6]

I had to confront this up close when I lived with my dying mother-in-law. We had dropped everything to be with her in Australia for her final weeks, which meant everything in our home, work and school life was in disarray. I was still trying to manage some of the mess from the other side of the world. But even as I tried to avoid the inevitable chaos, I was forced to face the reality around me. My mother-in-law had always been a hero of getting things done. One of the biggest parts of my grief was coming to terms with how many things she was forced to leave undone. To help her, I dug through closets—closets filled with projects that would never be finished. I knew if she'd had the energy to think about it, those incomplete things would have made her crazy,

> Liturgical time is essentially poetic time, oriented toward process rather than productivity, willing to wait attentively in stillness rather than always pushing to "get the job done."
> **Kathleen Norris**[7]

but she was forced to handle greater realities. There were other processes and messes and tensions she had no choice but to deal with.

I came home to the disorder of my own life and work and saw them with new eyes, with an understanding that when I died there would also be unfinished projects, unwritten letters, unanswered questions, unresolved conflicts in my closet and computer and heart. To learn to accept this unpleasant reality, I forced myself to leave the repetitive tasks of life incomplete, to leave one sock in the hamper, one glass in the sink. It goes against my desire to wipe my hands and be done, but it teaches me to accept the less-than-completeness of life.

> What do people gain from all their labors
>   at which they toil under the sun?
> Generations come and generations go,
>   but the earth remains forever.
> The sun rises and the sun sets,
>   and hurries back to where it rises.
> The wind blows to the south
>   and turns to the north;
> round and round it goes,
>   ever returning on its course.
> All streams flow into the sea,
>   yet the sea is never full.
> To the place the streams come from,
>   there they return again. (Ecclesiastes 1:3-7)

When we have that collision course with reality, will it shatter us? Or will the discomfort force us to ask questions we'd never have asked from the comfort of completion and clarity? Will waiting for answers force us to trust in the source of all knowledge? There are certainly tasks to be done and things for us to learn and people for us to develop in our work, but do we do them just to get them done? Or is there something to be found even in the process of getting them done? What do we break in the rush to resolution?

In our ministries, the best way to step toward this reality is just to acknowledge it as a truth. The best way to relieve the anxiety is just to admit to ourselves and each other that faith is a lifelong process of following, wrestling, growing. Once we set aside the frustration that we haven't yet arrived, all that energy can then be devoted to the following, wrestling and growing.

Reflect

When you find yourself unable to control or complete all you'd like to control or complete, how does it make you feel? Are there ways you're rushing to resolve something? How could you submit to the process and watch what God will do in it? As you develop and disciple others, how can you be patient with their process?

PLAYFUL

When was the last time you asked an adult, "So, how have you been playing lately?" Play is not something grownups talk about. We assume it's pointless and childish. But from play grows connectedness and community, creativity and joy. Stuart Brown, who has the enviable job of running the National Institute for Play, has devoted his life to the study of our human need for it. He writes, "Many of the things we regard as play may, on closer inspection, have the qualities of work. And what to many people might seem like work may really be built on a foundation of play. . . . The work that we find most fulfilling is almost always a recreation and extension of youthful play."[8] Which leads to the question of how we played as children, back when play was a kind of compulsion.

One of my childhood highlights was entering a songwriting contest for a children's radio program. After perfecting my magnum opus (which began, "In the middle of the night, when there's no one else in sight, my toothbrush comes alive, and starts to jive!"), I gathered my friends in the school music room and we recorded it, with Tammy on the xylophone and Charmayne on the tambourine and of course me, the composer, on vocals.

Making something is always fun, but even better is making something with others. Leading a church feels very much like that, and it's been a joy to name it. I have an idea and invite others into discovering together what it can become, whether it's creating a Sunday service or exploring how to express hospitality or figuring out how God is moving.

Since we're talking here about a playful culture for a team or community, it may also help to consider your family's play personality. In my family growing up, we often played together by exploring—a bookstore or town or forest. In my family now, we play by making up scenarios and stories that often begin with, "What would you do if . . . ?" or "Wouldn't it be funny if . . . ?" I bring that exploring and imagining to the decisions we make and the meetings I lead at UCC.

Reflect

How did you play as a kid? How do those play preferences show themselves in your work? How can you make the most of the parts of your work that make you come alive? What opportunities are there to invite others to play?

Like many churches, before services on Sunday we have a run-through for staff and volunteers to go over the plan for the day and pray. It's often filled with friendly teasing and lighthearted joking. There will be a comment about someone's shoes or an interpretation of the strange shape of the "circle" we've made when we join hands ("It's a prayer pickle!"). It's fun and a good place to be. But it's not by accident. That moment before the service can be intense—inevitably we have a technical problem or the band doesn't feel good about the new song. We choose to joke then to alleviate stress—many studies have shown the power of laughter. But we also joke to communicate something even deeper: that it's not about us. We choose to be playful because our performance is not the point, because even if we don't feel great about our readiness, God's ability to work is not wrapped up in our readiness. As eternally important as our work is, we of all people have reason to play because our work is not our work alone. The nice thing about this is that it works backward too. When we choose to be playful even if we don't feel like it—because we trust that God is at work—it's an act of faith, which teaches us more faith. So, you see, playfulness is serious business.[9]

COMFORTABLE IN UNCERTAINTY

It's a pastor's role to cast vision, to stretch the congregation to new places and fearlessly speak on God's behalf. But how can we really know what God wants? Of course, we know generally—he wants all people to be restored to him. But what does he think of our new discipleship program or the sanctuary renovations?

> When the brilliant ethicist John Kavanaugh went to work for three months at "the house of the dying" in Calcutta, he was seeking a clear answer as to how best to spend the rest of his life. On the first morning there he met Mother Teresa. She asked, "And what can I do for you?" Kavanaugh asked her to pray for him.
>
> "What do you want me to pray for?" she asked. He voiced the request that he had borne thousands of miles from the United States. "Pray that I have clarity."
>
> She said firmly, "No, I will not do that." When he asked her why, she said, "Clarity is the last thing you are clinging to and must let go of." When Kavanaugh commented that she always seemed to have the clarity he longed for, she laughed and said, "I have never had clarity; what I have always had is trust. So I will pray that you trust God."[10]

Early in my ministry I had a moment of "clarity." During a personal retreat, I had a strong sense of where God was leading our church. It was such a beautiful vision that I took it to the church, bubbling over with confidence and energy. I was met with faces that didn't understand. In my urgency to see the vision fulfilled, I used language like "This is God's will for us!"—which didn't help. People whose prayers and reflection didn't lead them to the same place felt manipulated by my God talk. But I lumbered on, fueled by my own vision, making grand claims. And things didn't go the way I'd promised.

After that experience, the next time I needed direction on a big ministry decision, I decided to leave God out of it. I'd made him look bad by abusing his name to get my way. I'd made promises of specific outcomes that must not have been from him, since they never materialized. So instead of seeking him, I switched into problem-solver mode. I took my carefully reasoned plan to the leadership and we shaped it and put it into place. It met or exceeded our goals and I got some pats on the back. But it felt small and godless.

When we seek God's leadership on big decisions, what do we expect him to provide? A five-year strategy? Is it enough for him to just reveal the next step? And when we step up in front of the eldership or the congregation to invite them into a new vision—maybe one we feel is directly from God himself—how do we do it? On the one hand, we want to dream big. But will we look dumb if the plan doesn't go as we promised? Will we make God look bad if we misspeak about where he is leading? Or will we make bold claims in his name and risk manipulating those who don't get the vision?

Scripture says, "Ask and you shall receive." That's pretty simple.

But not everyone in Scripture got what they asked for.

Even Jesus. His pleading in the Garden of Gethsemane is a deeply disturbing scene but one that offers insight into how to have confidence without clarity. This prayer can be a different model prayer, one for seeking clarity.

The prayer in Mark 14:36 can be broken down into three beautifully simple elements, and when we feel lost, a simple formula may be all we can handle.

"Abba, Father, everything is possible for you." What a way to start a prayer! It begins with a reminder of whom we're addressing. We're not filling out paperwork to submit to some faceless bureaucrat. This is our Father. And what a Father he is! Nothing is beyond him. There is no question about whether or not God can do what we're about to ask.

"Take this cup from me." Here's where Jesus presents his heart's desire. He's not afraid to be honest and admit he wants something. Five simple syllables never had so much significance. When we pray according to this model, what heartfelt yearning do we insert here? God already knows our heart, the ways we long to see restoration in our congregations and communities. So we might as well voice them. Even if doing so makes us feel the vulnerability of hope.

"Yet not what I will, but what you will." This final statement perfectly balances the prayer, making it a very brief but satisfying prayer to pray. We've acknowledged who God is and what he can do. We've been honest about our desires. And now we end by giving God the final word. We trust the outcome to a well-meaning, all-powerful being who has heard us.

Reflect

How are you seeking clarity? How can you insert your request into the middle of this Gethsemane prayer? How can you step forward into what is next without knowing the details of exactly where it will lead?

In all of the decisions we need to make as church leaders, this is a perfect prayer to pray. Years of praying this prayer have brought me to this simple statement—which my congregation is probably tired of hearing, but I'll keep saying it anyway: "I don't know what God *will* do, but I know what he *can* do."

It's not our job to know all the answers but to know the One who knows them. It's our job to faithfully lead our flock to follow him, even though we're not sure where he'll take us. As our people see our confidence even when we don't have clarity, they'll find the same confidence. Not in us but in him.[11]

When church leaders explore their own vulnerability and shape a culture from it, they invite others to find comfort in their own vulnerability. As leaders we don't have to be good at it before we begin but can learn it along with our communities. When we step into this together we learn peace with all that is outside of our power, peace with the mystery of God. We find new ways that the church can be whole and healthy.

Assessing Your Church Culture

To evaluate your church culture, you may want to ask Brené Brown's ten culture questions:

1. What behaviors are rewarded? Punished?
2. Where and how are people actually spending their resources (time, money, attention)?
3. What rules and expectations are followed, enforced and ignored?
4. Do people feel safe and supported talking about how they feel and asking for what they need?
5. What are the sacred cows? Who is most likely to tip them? Who stands the cows back up?
6. What stories are legend and what values do they convey?
7. What happens when someone fails, disappoints or makes a mistake?
8. How is vulnerability (uncertainty, risk and emotional exposure) perceived?
9. How prevalent are shame and blame and how are they showing up?
10. What's the collective tolerance for discomfort? Is the discomfort of learning, trying new things, and giving and receiving feedback normalized, or is there a high premium put on comfort (and how does that look)?[12]

8

Changing the Mold

How Vulnerable Pastors Recognize and Develop Leaders

To carry out an unscientific but entertaining poll, I often do an online image search and see what pops up. If you search for "Christian leader," you get lots of images of people on mountaintops with their arms raised. If you search for "church leader," you get lots of famous people (and a couple of mug shots). While of course the Internet and the collective human psyche are, thankfully, not yet synonymous, there is some overlap.

For another unscientific but entertaining poll, I went to the library and picked up the first leadership advice book I saw. According to my quick summary of the table of contents, here's what it takes to be a leader:

- Have confidence.
- Be prepared.
- Have courage.
- Be audacious.
- Be diligent.

- Be persistent.
- Be dedicated.
- Stay focused.
- Express passion.
- Have integrity.

Our culture's standard of leadership sets the bar pretty high. When we think "leader," we often visualize strong, otherworldly people. While we admire that kind of leader, very few of us are qualified to *be* it. And few biblical leaders would qualify either.

As I've already shared, my collision with limited models of leadership almost took me out. Being at that Christian conference made me suddenly and acutely aware of how very un-male, un-businesslike, un-American and un-extroverted I am. Maybe you are male, businesslike, American or extroverted. Maybe you're all four. So you may not collide with those models in the way I did. But you may have the lingering sense that your family is less together or your appetites are more shameful or your sermons are less impressive than they should be. I'd like to share the way I worked through my collision with the Christian leader norm, but let me first say this: My points of collision may not be yours and I share them to show how, with time, they became opportunities. I hope it helps you name your points of collision and the opportunities they hold for you.

COLLIDING WITH LEADERSHIP NORMS

We've been told that weak people can't lead, so every weakness feels like disqualification from leadership. Here's what my weakness has taught me about leadership.

Being a woman can feel like weakness. When you're a woman, your own body teaches you your limits. From the time you're small there is always someone bigger with a stronger body and a deeper voice. As you grow you learn how little control you have over your own body, from a sometimes painful, often embarrassing inconvenience that visits you every month to the strange season of having a person growing inside of you—one that for nine months does what it likes and takes what it needs. When the little bundle makes its appearance, your body goes from creator of life to sustainer of life, and all kinds of new systems kick into gear that, again, are beyond your control. Inhabiting this ever-changing form forces a woman to acknowledge (even celebrate) her limits and to know her responsibility to and increase her reliance on the broader community.

So if being a woman teaches humility and collaboration, isn't it a strength to be a woman?

In the church, these are leadership skills.

Being an artist can feel like weakness. If you're an artist, you're spurred on by an unending search for truth and beauty. Your breath is taken away by the smallest seemingly insignificant thing and you're unfit for anything but crying or singing or writing for the rest of the day. Once you've found a tiny sign of hope, you must make sense of it. And so you make things to process and express it, trying to capture all the feeling and meaning through the limited media of notes and words and paint. You step into a creative process that is sometimes cruel and raw, a little too close for comfort. Then with shaking hands you put that outpouring of your soul into a public form and hope someone understands.

If creative people know how to find truth and beauty even when it's hidden in brokenness, if they're comfortable with mystery, failure and vulnerability, isn't it a strength to be an artist?

In the church, these are leadership skills.

Being an outsider can feel like weakness. Being on the outside means always having that vague sense that you didn't get the inside joke. You feel like a child again as you learn things that are obvious to everyone else (how to ride the bus? how to turn on the shower? what is a "pinch hitter"?). But over time you compensate. You learn not only to speak but to listen in other languages. You become self-aware as those things that were once transparent about yourself (back when everyone around you was the same as you) are suddenly glaring. For the first time you feel the weight of the lens of your own culture, your own assumptions, and eventually you learn how to switch glasses.

If being displaced helps us relate to the ways God's people have always been sojourners, isn't it meaningful to be displaced? If outsiders know how to be flexible and self-aware, to communicate in many contexts, to identify with others also on a journey, isn't it a strength to be an outsider?

In the church, these are leadership skills.

Being an introvert can feel like weakness. Thinking of the perfect answer a day after the question was asked makes you feel dumb, even though your belated but perfectly worded response is more insightful than the one given by the quick thinker in the room. Needing to recover from extended periods with people draws labels like "antisocial," even though you may have great social skills. Longing for depth and complexity and silence makes you feel like a precious egghead in a world hungry for sound bites and noise.

If introverts know how to listen and are unafraid of silence, depth and authenticity, isn't it a strength to be an introvert?

In the church, these are leadership skills.

In whatever way you feel you don't measure up to the leader norm—you think your past disqualifies you or you're too young or too weird or too hounded by sin—what will you do with the gap between who you are and who you believe you should be? Will it be a point of shame and disqualification? Or will it drive you closer to God? Will you see in it an opportunity to learn your deep need? Anything that drives us to know what we lack, to know our dependence, is an opportunity for ministry. When we see our own weakness as a ministry resource, we have unlimited resources!

Reflect

How do you collide with the norms of Christian leadership? Are you not good or smart or popular or healthy or normal or quick or deep or sinless enough? How can your points of collision become opportunities?

FINDING UNLIKELY LEADERS

How did we get to this place in contemporary leadership thinking where we would fail to recognize the potential in a young David or a tormented Paul or a timid Esther? Their deep need for and reliance on God made them leaders. When leadership grows out of a deep need for God's leadership, it takes on a very different face. And if leadership means trusting God in the midst of need, it opens the ranks to many more than the strong and highly gifted. Once we've learned how to lead from our own need, the urgency of our mission leaves us no choice but to discover that potential in others and develop them in it. Not only will this bring joy to those who don't see their own leadership potential, it brings life and diversity to the body of Christ. At a time when the church is in danger of losing its voice in the world, how much more refreshing will our message be when we speak through a multitude of new voices!

In light of these truths, many Christian authors are calling for a broader model of leadership. Rex Miller explains that for the past sixty years, organizations have rewarded "skills like persuasion, a high-profile image, innovation, risk taking . . . leaps up the success ladder, interpersonal skills, the ability to think on one's feet, and so forth. . . . [But] congregants in the emerging . . . culture are hungry for leaders who are approachable, . . . transparent, and real. They want to connect with someone who is unscripted, unrehearsed, and not 'on.'"[1]

Adam S. McHugh shares his own story: "I subconsciously believed that ministers and other Christian leaders needed a certain set of personality traits in order to thrive in ministry. . . . My struggles to be an introverted pastor are representative of the struggles many introverts face when navigating the waters of Christian community, which can be unintentionally, or intentionally, biased toward extroversion."[2]

Alan Hirsch and Dave Ferguson call churches to invite more

female and right-brained ways of thinking into leadership, concluding by saying that "movements need 'masculine' technique and structure, certainly, but they also require us to be more fluid, responsive, and intuitive in order to develop—especially when we need creative solutions in order to thrive/survive."[3] A broader model of leadership will mean that we suddenly have more leaders than we thought, will reflect more fully the personality of Christ's church, allowing that complex and diverse church to reach our complex and diverse world.

The church is ready for some contrary thinking on leadership, to challenge assumptions that may not be scriptural or right for our era. Which is why I've found a great resource in *The Contrarian's Guide to Leadership* by Stephen B. Sample.[4] In opening our eyes to alternative ways to lead, Sample opens the gates to a multitude of passionate people who may not recognize their leadership potential. Without maligning traditional ways of leading, his book empowers leaders to see the world differently, to be a little more creative or philosophical or slower to make decisions than the leadership types we usually see. As such it is a great tool for artists, introverts, women, intellectuals and anyone who questions their ability to lead because they don't fit the usual model, helping them to see that they bring something unique to the organizations they lead.[5]

Since there are many potential leaders who don't see their leadership potential, the onus is on us to invite them, and to invite them well. I've seen efforts to do this that were well-intentioned but not carried out well. One such example is an event I attended that finished with this message: "You might see these big names on stage, but leadership is not just for authors and megachurch pastors. God calls many to leadership. If you feel called to leadership, gather for a special leaders' lunch today!" When I later passed by the leaders' lunch, all the expected people were there—

and they should have been—but there were many people who *weren't* there: people who wouldn't self-select for leadership, people who had never seen a leader who looked or thought like them, people who had never been told they could lead, people who had been told they *shouldn't* lead. When I say the onus is on us, it's not only on us to invite them but to track them down, tell them what we see in them, champion them, remind them what we see in them, walk alongside them as they try and fail and try again. Our job is to invite them and keep inviting them.

To be honest, I'm a little wary of people who say they want to be leaders. Most great leaders I know didn't choose to be leaders; they were motivated by what felt at first like insurmountable obstacles, personal baggage or frustration with the status quo. And as they worked through their own stuff, they figured out something worth sharing. I was never the kind of writer who decided I wanted to write and then went on adventures to find something to write about. In fact, I wasn't a writer at all. I had things burning a hole in my head, so I had no choice but to find a way to communicate them. I was never the kind of leader who wanted to lead. I had things to say that I wished someone had said to me, things to be that I wished someone had been to me, so I had no choice but to figure out a way to say and be them.

So if leadership sometimes emerges from angst and weakness, frustration and obstacles, where are we looking for emerging leaders? The one with the easy answers and the easy smile might dazzle us at first, but are we overlooking the awkward, the quiet, the odd and the artsy? Some of the best leaders I know were overlooked because they had a problem with authority or asked uncomfortable questions or tripped over their own tongues. Undoubtedly giftedness is good, and when equipped with a heart for service and a sense of personal need, a gifted leader is golden. But since giftedness has the potential to get in the way of a heart of service and sense of need, if I had to choose, I'd rather take a broken, selfless servant who needed to work on her communication skills than a vibrant preacher who had no need for God.

Let me tell you about a few leaders I know who didn't know they were leaders.

Jen is a young mother who can at any moment provide a humorously self-effacing and detailed list of her own limitations. Ask her for her strengths and she'll probably mention the speed with which she can list her weaknesses. She's easily overwhelmed by tasks and emotions, and she often feels disorganized. But she's overwhelmed because she sees so much and cares so much. Her house may be in disarray, but her kids are kind and creative. Because they have been around her their whole lives.

When Jen stepped into leadership of our missions team, she felt like she was in over her head and often wondered what on earth she was doing. She had no ability to set up a new ministry, make decisions, motivate people or organize systems. But when I reminded her that missions is not about programs but relationships and taking Jesus to those who need him, she began to see things differently—that instead of disqualifying her, her sensitivity to others, her self-awareness and her insight make her highly valued as a missions leader. The things that feel to her like weakness—her awareness of her own failings, her willingness to laugh at herself, her comfort with her own humanity— these are the very traits that invite others into the mess of working in a mission that's over our heads.

Dwayne is an ex-convict and recovering addict who wrestles with bipolar disorder. Some of his past choices have left their mark on his life and I get the feeling sometimes that they're still nipping at his heels. So he knows his deep need for a Savior. It drives him to trust in God every moment and forces him to rely on his Christian community. It motivates him to reach out, with great compassion, to those who are where he once was, often at the risk of his own safety. When he works and sings and preaches, I see he is not working in his own strength. It's a beautiful thing to see.

Hannah is a young woman in campus ministry. She takes time finding her words and often hangs back when there is someone else more confident in the group. She is often aware of how she doesn't measure up but never more than when she sees how much she could know and experience God. She longs to live in him but is acutely aware of how little she understands. She regrets choices from her past and fears that their shadow still lingers. But when she hears about the same fears in others, she speaks with passion, granting them grace and spurring them on to goodness. Although she feels far from God, when we look in her face, we can see that she knows him and speaks from her own experience of his presence.

I don't think one of these wonderful people would have gone to that lunch for leaders. People like this rarely put themselves forward; they wait for the people of God to see something in them. So when we do see something in them, we must call it out and annoy them with it. We need to say, "I see this in you." And, "I've been where you are." And when they tentatively try something new, we need to say, "How did that feel? What did you learn? Don't give up." They need a note that says, "Thinking of you today as you preach!" or "How was it to lead your first meeting?"

Reflect

Who in your community knows their need for God? How could they be leaders?

We often confuse encouragement with compliments. But if we want to ensure that a movement doesn't end with us, we must embrace a kind of purposeful encouragement, one that is not optional. How can we look for opportunities to praise? Not for the sake of puffing up egos but to point out the good God has put in his people for the sake of his church? When a child finally does the thing her parents have been waiting for, the best parents do a little dance all around it, and the child is so delighted that she wants to do it again. How can we do a little dance around anything that looks like leadership, any way that someone displays a gift or takes on the mission or follows the call? If someone has sparked something good in us or our community, how can we return that good to them?

In my own experience, I received specific words from brothers and sisters in Christ that I wrote down and still return to often. These have been the difference between knowing the way forward and giving up. They are words like "I see Christ in you" or "Don't give up; God has a purpose" or "Something you did revealed truth to me" or "Keep using that gift—it's a blessing to the church." How can we be like Paul, spurring his young leaders on to good works, calling out the gifts among the fellowship of believers?

It's not enough just to give leadership opportunities to emerging leaders. They need us to walk alongside them, process the challenges and frustrations with them, help them recognize the lessons and possibilities. Too often, when we realize we're hogging all the leadership, in our efforts to share it we dump emerging leaders in the deep end, skipping the long and painful process of developing them, bypassing what's often called the "leadership pipeline." There are plenty of resources about the stages of leadership development and they've been helpful to me.[6] But one of the most memorable examples of leadership in my life came from a very unlikely place.

I was in that groggy state you can only reach on a flight across the Pacific. You know you've reached it when you'll watch reality TV just to make the time pass. So I found myself watching the UK edition of *What*

Not to Wear. (Okay, if I'm honest, I was actually enjoying it.) The hosts, Trinny and Susannah, were doing their usual thing, explaining to their guest the best clothing for different body types. When they tried to describe the ways jeans fit around hips, they found words too limiting, so they did something unexpected—they whipped off their own jeans and stood in their underwear to show exactly what they were talking about. I'm sure there was an element of showmanship going on—it's good for ratings if the hosts strip down to their undies.

But in an industry that's all about looking good, it takes some courage to show the specific ways you don't look good. Certainly Trinny and Susannah are attractive and healthy women, but when they grabbed pieces of their own flesh and said, "See this jiggly bit?" we could say, "Um, yes." They're TV presenters, not swimsuit models. In fact, they're anti-models. A model stands at a distance and says, "You should be like me. Even though we all know that's not going to happen." Instead, these women were willing to be vulnerable in order to show that no one is perfect, not even TV personalities. In light of all the negative stereotypes and unattainable beauty ideals that women face, this small act was a step in the right direction, a step that cost something. I may not reference these hosts often as leadership models, but there are many times when I'm opening my own life to those I lead that I remember that surprising reality TV scene.

Thankfully, our roles rarely call on us to bare our nakedness in a literal way. But as we develop those who are one step behind us, how do we welcome them into where we are in all its ordinariness? Are we willing to admit to our associate that our sermon just isn't coming together? And even ask him to give input? Are we willing to start a meeting by saying, "I'm worn out. Could I ask you to pray for me?" I never feel like doing it. In fact, I hate doing it. But I choose to keep doing it because from it I've seen how the church can be the church, gathering around me, offering prayer and support.

Even more than that, I've watched leaders realize they're leaders. They've seen that having a bad day (or week, or year) doesn't disqualify us. They've seen that feeling stuck or confused or overwhelmed doesn't disqualify us. They've seen that wrestling with personal issues and questioning God doesn't disqualify us. They can say, "If Mandy can do it, anyone can!" It's the kind of leadership model I need, so it's the kind of leadership model I'm choosing to be.

Reflect

How could you share leadership more and walk alongside emerging leaders as they learn? How could your transparency create a new, attainable model of leadership for others?

9

Taking Our
Own Sweet Time

How Vulnerable Pastors Use Their Time and Energy

> *To allow oneself to be carried away by*
> *a multitude of conflicting concerns, to surrender to too*
> *many demands, to commit oneself to too many projects, to want*
> *to help everyone in everything, is to succumb to violence.*

Thomas Merton, *Conjectures of a Guilty Bystander*

The choices we make about using our time and energy are often knee-jerk reactions—long-lived ruts where we repeatedly do whatever it takes to avoid failure. Some of my biggest failures have been failures to live up to my own expectations, and in some ways failing ourselves is the hardest failure, because our own expectations follow us everywhere we go. If we stopped long enough to assess our expectations, we might not even know where we picked them up. But to assess our expectations for ourselves, we have to be conscious of them.

I've shared how I've collided with the expectations of others. It's even more surprising and painful to collide with your own ideals, to find you're not living up even to what *you* think you should be. After one particularly painful disappointment in our long attempt to move back to Australia, I plunged into depression. I was depressed because I took responsibility for the disappointing situation. I should have seen it coming, thought of other possibilities, worked harder. Then everything would have fallen into place and the ground would not now be falling out from under me. This self-accusation was the way I'd talked to myself my whole life, but this time something was different. This time my life was in pieces and, like Job, I sat among the potsherds. As I worked to piece my life back together, I stopped with each fragment and asked, "Do I really want this in my life?" Some pieces didn't make the cut.

One piece that got left on the scrap heap was what I call "shoulding on myself."[1] To get them outside of myself so I could look them in the eye, I made a list of my "shoulds." (I didn't realize until I started this book how many points of healing have come from making lists!) The list went something like this:

- I should always do whatever is necessary to have a good relationship with God.

- I should always do whatever is necessary to have a good relationship with my family.

- I should always get everything on my to-do list done (including everything on this list).

- I should never forget anything.

- I should always do everything to the best of my ability.

- I should always be pleasant.

- I should always look put together.

- I should be well-read.

- I should always keep my house clean and organized.

- I should ensure my kids are always well-behaved and well-adjusted.
- I should not burden others with my feelings or needs.
- I should always say yes when others ask for help.
- I should exercise every day.
- I should be well-informed about current events.
- I should have guests for dinner regularly (and all food should be made from scratch).
- I should give my kids every possible opportunity.
- I should be very involved at my kids' school and know the names of all the parents of my kids' friends.
- I should be very involved in my neighborhood and know the names of my neighbors' pets.
- I should get everything in one trip to the store and not have to go back midweek.
- I should be joyful and fulfilled.

  Ugh!

  My life had been lived in the space between these "shoulds" for so long that I had come to believe I was comfortable contorted into the shape they forced me to take. Now that I have extracted that framework from my life and recovered a more healthy posture, the "shoulds" are repulsive to me. As you can see, some of them are actually at odds with each other. I never consciously decided that this made a well-balanced and healthy list of expectations. But wherever they came from, they weren't kind to me. So for the first time I was able to release myself from some of them. Which also meant lowering my standards—a lot.

  Our culture tells us, "Look at all the things that need to be done (oh, and by the way, here are a few dozen things you haven't thought of that you should include) and decide how to spend your time and energy based on how much needs to be done. Did we mention that everyone else manages it somehow?" Instead I decided to list my "shoulds" in order of priority—after scratching out or rewording the ones that were just ridiculous. Then I started at the top and began doling out time and energy, and when I got to the place in the list where the time and energy ran out, I stopped giving time and energy.

It was revolutionary! It stopped somewhere between "I should exercise every day" and "I should be well-informed about current events." Which are both good and important things. It's humbling to see that, even after you've cleared out the worthless "shoulds," there are valuable things on the list that you just can't get to, or at least not as often as you'd like. So I made a plan to exercise every other day and I subscribed to a weekly current affairs magazine. And I admitted that there are some things I value that just won't get any of my time, at least for this season of my life. One of the hardest things about this process was that we used to invite people for dinner most weeks. These days, because of the nature of our ministries and the ages of our children, we have energy to do it (and be present and pleasant) only about once a month.

Reflect

What are your "shoulds"? Are they kind? Or reasonable? Share them with a trusted friend and ask him or her to help you rework them, bearing in mind that your "shoulds" may change with seasons of life.

In a culture built on consumerism and productivity, it can feel like the world wants to get as much out of us as it can—our time, energy, money. So we have to recognize that dehumanizing force for what it is and step out of it. It will take determination to be countercultural and it will take courage to keep returning to healthy practices when others around us interpret our choices as personal rejection, laziness or selfishness. We need allies who are stepping out of the rat race of hyperproductivity to remind us we're not crazy or alone. To be one friend in that effort, let me share a few ways I'm stepping toward healthier practices.

LIMITING ADVERTISEMENTS

I'm convinced every ad agency has a "should" specialist. This person knows all about human inadequacy and that there are dollars connected to how much we feel it. He or she drives us to feel it, not to direct us to God but to direct us to the product at hand. The "should" specialist begins with the fundamental truth of our humanness, then tells us the lie that we can dominate it. Flip through any magazine and you'll see what I'm talking about. The underlying message for almost any ad is "You feel inadequate and powerless. Here's a way to control it, numb it or overcome it." Whether it's playing on our powerlessness about retirement, hair loss, weight gain or getting our kids to eat healthy food, it's a subtle message that weakness of any kind should not be tolerated. (An even more subtle message is that you're the only one who feels the weakness.)

Reflect

How are you most exposed to and undermined by advertising? How can you limit your exposure to it?

LEARNING BY DISCOMFORT

There's something inherent in a "should" that communicates that it's not optional. So pinpoint the "shoulds" that your rational side knows are the most unhealthy or unreasonable, and just stop doing them, even if your compulsive self starts writhing. It may half-kill you at first, but it may be just what you need—you'll see that your colleagues won't lose all respect for you if you haven't read that latest book or your spouse won't leave if you need to be yourself today. Maybe being comfortable with the fact you haven't read that important book will provide an opportunity for you to ask your colleague to share what he thought of it. Maybe being yourself for a day will give your spouse an opportunity to minister to you. You may be surprised that the thing you avoided at all costs has happened and the world has not crumbled around your ears.

Reflect

Look back on the list of "shoulds" you made earlier. Choose one that's unhealthy and just stop doing it. (If it affects other people in your life, you may want out of kindness to give them some notice.) Were the ramifications as bad as you expected?

KNOWING OUR NEEDS

Our work is not just what we do. How we are is a big part of it. Our ministries won't last long if we snap the head off every person who asks us to do something. When I first began my ministry I applied the world's approach to work, which meant I was a machine that got tasks done. *Pray with single mother (check!). Schedule the volunteers (check!). Plan staff retreat (check!).* I got plenty done, but at what cost? I knew part of my role was to be nice to everyone at church, so I saved my tiredness and frustration for my family. Around this time 1 Corinthians 13 hit me in a new way: If I'm getting a million tasks done in God's name but not doing them with love, what good am I? And even if I feel love for people but I'm too tired to treat them with love, what good is that? This reading of Corinthians became a moment to ask myself, *What do I need so I can actually express my love? What needs to be true in my life to allow me to be emotionally and spiritually present for my church and my family?* Sleep was top of the list. A balanced diet, regular exercise, time for fun. After that, a few more "shoulds" had to get cut.

We must be doing something wrong if doing church means ruining health and families. J.R. Briggs in his book *Fail* lists a depressing set of statistics of the toll ministry takes on pastors, including the fact that 50 percent of pastors' marriages end in divorce, 80 percent of pastors say ministry has adversely affected their families and 45 percent of pastors say they've experienced depression or burnout to the extent that they needed to take a leave of absence.[2] We would say we believe that God cares about our bodies and our families as well as our churches. So why do we accept the idea that he wants us to run church in a way that destroys us? God has commissioned humans to run his church. Do we think he doesn't know our limitations? There must be some way for us to do his work as humans.

I don't know the answer, but I do see that the churches that wear people out the most often have an attractional church model.[3] I don't know if part of the answer involves leaning more missional. Or limiting the number of big events we host. Or promoting some of our volunteers to real positions of leadership (instead of just numbers for our paid staff to manage). Or keeping our churches purposefully small and local. Or having realistic expectations of ourselves. Or changing what we measure. Or some combination of all of the above.

Reflect

What do you need so that you can express genuine love in your home and work? What needs to be true in your life to allow you to be emotionally and spiritually present for your church and family? How can facing your own human limitations be an opportunity to trust that God cares about your needs as much as he cares about the needs of those you serve?

NURTURING AND PROTECTING CREATIVE ENERGY

Our work requires us to dig deep into our emotional and creative re-sources, the kind of energy that can't be forced. My best ideas usually come in the shower or on a walk, not when I'm sitting at my computer. So I embrace that. Sermon-writing day often includes making soup because the calming rhythm of chopping invites reflection. When ideas come, no matter what I'm doing, I go with that energy while I have it (which often means I'm working on a sermon for next month because an idea came to me while I still don't have an idea for this week's message).

There's something to learn from the work practices of creative people. Creatives learn to be flexible and responsive, are kind to them-selves, listen to their own energy, make time for joy. But you don't have to call yourself a creative to manage your creative energy as they do. How could you incorporate a few of their practices?

- Daydream.
- Observe everything.
- Work the hours that work for you.
- Take time for solitude.
- Turn obstacles around.
- Seek new experiences.
- "Fail up."
- Ask big questions.
- People-watch.
- Follow your passions.
- Take risks.
- Get out of your own head.
- Lose track of time.
- Surround yourself with beauty.
- Constantly shake things up.
- Take time for mindfulness.[4]

CREATING HEALTHY RHYTHMS OF LIFE

Another way to create expectations on a human scale is to create rhythms of life. While the idea of "ritual" can seem rote and mean-ingless, I love the metaphor of rhythm. A rhythm doesn't dictate the entire piece of music but creates a steady framework on which music

can be made. We see throughout Scripture that God himself insti-
tuted daily, weekly and annual rhythms of life to assure and shape his
people. To remind us of the story we're in, he created practices that
engage human minds, muscles and senses to engage whole selves.

If every time you went to the
grocery store it was rearranged, it
would take twice as long and be
twice as tiring to find everything.
This is how life can feel if every day
we have to make decisions about
how to use the day. But when the
store layout is the same, you naturally find yourself thinking about
rice right after you've been thinking
about beans because the order is familiar. So, ironically, when we have
a framework (but not a rigid, in-
flexible schedule) we have freedom,
a kind of liturgy of life. As Jim
Loehr and Tony Schwartz write,

> Rituals provide a stable
> framework in which creative
> breakthroughs often occur. They
> can also open up time for re-
> covery and renewal, when rela-

[Harnessing fire, building the pyra-
mids and discovering penicillin] required some plain old-fashioned
stick-to-itiveness. But the insight that
led to them probably came from the
daydreaming mode. This brain state,
marked by the flow of connections
among disparate ideas and thoughts,
is responsible for our moments of
greatest creativity and insight, when
we're able to solve problems that
previously seemed unsolvable. You
might be going for a walk or grocery
shopping or doing something that
doesn't require sustained attention
and suddenly—boom—the answer
to a problem that had been vexing
you suddenly appears. This is the
mind-wandering mode, making connections among things that we
didn't previously see as connected.
Daniel J. Levitin[5]

tionships can be deepened and spiritual reflection becomes
possible. The limitations of conscious will and discipline are
rooted in the fact that every demand on our self-control—from
deciding what we eat to managing frustration, from building
an exercise regimen to persisting at a difficult task—all draw on
the same easily depleted reservoir of energy.[6]

> ## *Reflect*
>
> How have ideas come to you when you've been doing something that didn't look like work? How could you create a work pattern that allows for the ebb and flow of human energy?

I admit that I can be a ritual fanatic. I believe so strongly in the power of ritual that I panic if my day doesn't look as it should, if we go to bed without praying one day. But this is the beauty of ritual. We are not checking off to-do lists but embracing lifestyle practices. So if I forget something or have to shuffle my week around, it doesn't ruin the long-term plan because I have something to return to.

I know that pastors are secretly curious about how other pastors spend their time. So, in case you're curious, here's how my week looks:[7]

- Monday: Sabbath (sleeping, writing, reading, walking, wasting time, having tea with a friend, shopping, making something). Lunch with my husband, Jamie.

- Tuesday: Working at the church, meetings with staff (service planning, vision casting, decision making, one-on-one encouragement, leadership development), emails, administrative tasks, one-time meetings with church and community members.

- Wednesday: Working from home on big-picture stuff (writing sermons, reading, listening to God), maybe a walk, cooking, laundry, groceries.

- Thursday: Working at the church (prayer group, volunteering at our café, one-time meetings with church and community members or networking with other leaders), evening church business or prayer meeting.

- Friday: Early-morning discipleship group, then whatever didn't get done that week, including prep for Sunday. Pizza night with the family!
- Saturday: Day off! Sleep in! Invite someone to the house or go somewhere fun. Usually just hang out around the house, read, make things, watch movies.
- Sunday: Early-morning walk, prayer, church, lunch, nap. Look forward to day off on Monday.

Within those weekdays, I have daily habits. Most weekdays at 6:20 a.m. our family is around the table, sipping tea and reading the Moravian text (usually grudgingly and groggily). And most weekdays around 7:30 a.m. I'm walking my dog and praying. Most afternoons at 3 p.m. I'm picking up kids from school, by 6:30 we're all around the table again and by 8:30 we're praying together to begin the process of wrapping up the day. By 10 p.m. (on a good day) I'm in bed falling asleep while trying to read that important book that just isn't getting read.

You may notice I don't spend regular one-on-one time with many church members. I invest that kind of regular personal attention in my (paid and lay) leaders, who then spend time one-on-one with church members. My other regular meetings with people are usually in groups. I will meet one-on-one once or twice with an individual who isn't staff or a leader but will then either invite that person into one of my groups, encourage him or her to find a personal mentor or ask the person to join another group. Discipleship training organization 3DM has helped me see that Jesus invested most of his time in twelve people and rarely met with them one-on-one.[8]

You may also notice that there aren't many extracurricular kids' activities. In addition to all the other limitations I've had to embrace, I've been humbled by my inability to keep pace with kids' activities and have had many conversations with my kids about that.[9] I want to

teach my children the lessons I'm learning about "shoulds." I want to
have human-scale expectations for them and for them to have human-
scale expectations for themselves. Dropping some "shoulds" may cost
something. What if my kids don't have the most impressive résumés
(when did kids start talking about their résumés in eighth grade
anyway?) but they're some of the most well-adjusted, creative,
thoughtful and interesting people to apply for college? Or better yet,
what if they're some of the most well-adjusted, creative, thoughtful
and interesting parents or neighbors?[10]

You may also notice how little I get done in my week. I'm only
discipling two regular groups. I'm not having multiple weeknight
meetings. I just can't. And I'm learning to be okay with that. Because
it forces me to ask others to do the things I can't. And they have the
blessing of using their gifts and watching God at work through their
weaknesses. It also means I have the same expectations for staff and
don't require them to work to the detriment of their health or marriage. My ideal is to hire people who are passionate about the work
I'm hiring them to do so I don't have to motivate them. Instead it's
often my job to tell them to take a break.

I'm frequently ashamed of how little I accomplish. But I haven't
always felt that shame. One of the hardest things for me about living in
the United States, even compared to Britain and Australia, is the pace
of life and constant striving. In Australia, everything stops at 10 a.m. and
3 p.m. for morning and afternoon tea. Even at school we had "little
lunch"—a fifteen-minute break at 10 a.m. In Britain, many workplaces
have traditionally had a "tea lady" who takes a cart of treats around to
workers. When you live in a context where everyone stops, not just every
year for a vacation but every day for a cup of tea, it's normal to need a
break. Rest is a normal part of the culture in many places. But often in
the US rest is a sign of failure—in fact, some companies are now trying
a policy of unlimited vacations and employees still aren't taking them![11]

I don't say this to complain about my second home but to give grace to my American friends. If you're worn out, maybe it's time to look at the cultural norms you're embracing, at the opportunities Christians have to speak comfort into this culture. People talk about "work-life balance," but that sounds like what bosses say to make you think they value your life outside of work just enough that you'll keep working. What if instead we talked about abundant life? Something is wrong when we become machines, when our time use is determined by how much there is to do. It means we're stressed so we can't sleep so we spend the day fueled by caffeine but we don't have time to exercise to release the stress so we yell at our kids and because of all the caffeine we can't sleep at night again. But at least we're getting our work done! How well and for how long? This doesn't sound like work on a human scale.

I'm not showing you my week because I think I've arrived. But I've submitted myself to this weekly schedule because I know it's what I'm capable of and it allows me to give my best attention to the most important things. I could probably do twice as much in a week but not with much real attentiveness. And not for very long. This is what I can do week after week. I'm painfully aware every week of how little I accomplish. I confess it to embrace my humanity and to encourage you to consider your own week, with humanity in mind.

> In our own contemporary context of the rat race of anxiety, the celebration of Sabbath is an act both of resistance and alternative. It is resistance because it is a visible insistence that our lives are not defined by the production and consumption of commodity goods. . . . It is an alternative to the demanding, chattering, pervasive presence of advertising and its great liturgical claim of professional sports that devour all our "rest time." The alternative on offer is the awareness and practice of the claim that we are situated on the receiving end of the gifts of God.
> **Walter Brueggemann**[12]

Reflect

Write up your weekly schedule. Do you have the time and energy for it week after week or is it a lifestyle that will lead to a breakdown? We all have crazy weeks and busy seasons of the year, but what would it take to make a weekly schedule that would be sustainable, even enjoyable? (We may have to patiently lead our elders or church leaders to help them see the cultural problem or they may interpret our choices as laziness. It may mean describing for lay leaders from different fields the unique challenges of pastoral work.) How can you be more fully present in what you do, even if it means getting less done?

SABBATH KEEPING

Let me finish with the most central ritual of all: sabbath keeping. It is the key to learning comfort with our humanity. If you want to begin anywhere, begin with sabbath. This stepping away from performance and accomplishment is so countercultural that I need a regular practice to ground me in it.

A few years ago, for Lent, I started a simple but for me extreme new practice. I decided to take a lunch break every workday. And because I knew it would be a challenge for me to override my Protestant work ethic, I set a recurring alarm. Every day at noon, no matter what I was doing, I had to stop and see to the basic human needs I had been ignoring in order to do my oh-so-important work. It was to be rest for the sake of rest, not for the sake of being more efficient when I returned to the work.

In the beginning, when the alarm chimed, I was well overdue for water, food and a trip to the bathroom. Over time I began to anticipate the break, and after the forty days I couldn't bring myself to turn off that annoying but wise alarm. So for the rest of the year it pinged at me every noon. Some days I gloated at it: "I know; I've already eaten!" Other days I cursed the pinging because I was right in the middle of saving the world.

Surprisingly, a year of obligatory lunch breaks taught my soul one of its best lessons: I have little power and that's okay. Walking away from writing that email—which I was sure would resolve every question in the mind of the recipient—prompted me to acknowledge that I'm not the only force at work in that person's life. Setting aside a project halfway through taught me a new comfort with incompleteness. Stopping to feel my dry mouth, my gurgling stomach, my screaming bladder instructed me, from my urges up, how mortal I am.

That same year my life included international dealings with estranged family members, the long, complicated illness and passing of my mother-in-law, major transitions in my workplace—plenty of opportunities to face incompleteness and mortality. With each challenge I discovered a surprising peace that a greater power was at work and a new ability to embrace the process until answers came. Here is one more way that, in learning my weakness, I have found strength. My heart no longer flutters at the slightest sign of instability and my stomach churns a little less when I'm not in control. I guess there are some things you can only learn by (not) doing.[13]

While I turned off the lunchtime alarm and now take a full day of sabbath, you don't have to start there. If you can just take ten minutes a day at first, do it. Let the rest fall in the middle of your work—there's a lesson in resting amidst busyness. And as you rest, tell yourself, "I'm not resting to be more productive but because I'm a human being. God delights in me, even though I'm not producing anything." When God released his people from slavery in Egypt, even before he gave the Ten Commandments, he gave them sabbath to break them out of the slave habit. Slaves don't get a break. But children do. Sabbath reminds us we are children of God.

At first sabbath keeping for me was just taking a break. Then it began to teach me comfort with my own humanity. And as I've continued in my practice of it, it has reshaped my entire ministry, redefining my goals and ideals of success. Since the definition of success is such a pressing issue in ministry today, let's explore what sabbath can bring to that conversation.

Reflect

If you already take a regular sabbath, are there ways you can make it even more of an opportunity to receive God's delight in you, even when you're not producing anything? If you don't already take a sabbath, how could you begin to make room for it?

10

Thriving for Others

How Vulnerable Pastors Measure Success

O ur church is located next to Cincinnati's College-Conservatory of Music. It's an interesting thing to disciple students in a performance-driven field. And it's fascinating to watch the dynamics from the outside, given that I'm also in what can become a performance-driven field.

Among all the music students we've encountered over the years, one has stood out. Ben was a highly successful musician who seemed almost untouched by performance pressure. He was motivated by pure love for music and was not above playing various styles in various venues—not too proud to play with amateurs in our worship band. He loved listening to others play, even the kids he took the time to teach. And when we watched him play, it was hard to tell how much of our joy came from the sound he produced and how much from the joy we saw in him. His peers would comment on the difference, remembering the joy they'd experienced before music became all about auditions and positions, back when they just loved the music. Ironically, although Ben cared less about success than many of his fellow students, he has gone on to make a successful living as a musician.

If we're honest, we can relate. We still strive personally and as congregations to be "something" on the outside. But what does it cost us on the inside? Much has been written in recent years about metrics of ministry success—models that count the three Bs (buildings, bodies and budgets) and the ways we work toward efficiency, calculability, predictability and control.[1] Even outside the church, questions are being raised about the effectiveness of these types of metrics in general, since "people whose performance is being measured will neglect other parts of their job just to focus on boosting the relevant numbers."[2] It's healthy that church leaders are reassessing how they count and define success.

In many of these conversations, we find that the way forward is faithfulness.[3] This has been an incredible encouragement to me, taking my focus from external elements that are outside of my control to internal elements over which I have a choice. Faithfulness takes our eyes from the surface level and draws them to health and deeper motivations. Just as you can get good grades without learning anything or being honest, you can increase the three Bs without being healthy or having the character of God. You can't fake faithful.

As I work to apply this new approach, asking myself each day whether I am being faithful, I encounter new questions: How do we become faithful? How do we remain faithful? And how do we decide how, where and when to apply those faithful efforts? Is it okay to look up from our faithful work and check the results to determine if we're using our energies well? We've set aside striving for success for the sake of success, but are there still external factors we should watch?

Arianna Huffington has contributed something new to the conversation of success—the idea of thriving. Her book *Thrive* recounts how she was successful according to traditional measures of success: money and power. But she was not "living a successful life by any sane definition of success."[4] This realization led her to ask the question that has been asked through the ages—"What is the good life?"—

which brings to mind Jesus' theme of abundant life: a fullness, not just a big number. Huffington's answers to that question led her to create a metric made up of four pillars: well-being, wisdom, wonder and giving. Perhaps our ministries could benefit from conversations that arise from the question "What is abundant life?" A shift of attention from success to thriving opens new possibilities for work like ours because it attends to health.

Reflect

What is the abundant life for you and your congregation? How are you moving toward it? How are your well-being, wisdom, wonder and giving?

Thriving is a beautiful word because it reminds us of the language Jesus uses. If God's love really is powerful, then when people encounter it they will naturally experience growth of some kind—thriving things grow and bear fruit and reproduce. It may not be in the form of attendance numbers, but if we're inviting the Spirit, we should expect his fruit. It may come in unexpected ways, so we can't set our own rigid agendas. But watching where and when and how it grows helps us make decisions. If I am a faithful farmer, how will I know if today requires watering or mulching? While I may not gather scientific statistics, if I'm in tune with my plants, I only have to be among them to see wilting or flourishing. Attending to health helps us decide where to apply our faithfulness: what needs faithful encouragement, faithful admonition, faithful prayer.

These are the results we look for and the stories of thriving we gather at UCC. But much of the broader church's focus on success and efficiency has come from the business world. And when you have a business within your ministry (albeit a nonprofit café), it makes you extra careful not to be the kind of shopkeeper-pastors Eugene Peterson warns about, concerned with "how to keep the customers happy, how to lure customers away from competitors down the street, how to package the goods so that the customers will lay out more money."[5] Is there a way to look for signs of life and growth, to hope we stay alive, maybe even grow, while still trying to give ourselves away?

Twelve years ago, our church transformed its fellowship hall into the city's first fair-trade café in order to welcome and bless our neighbors. And we have undoubtedly done that. But two years ago we closed the café for Christmas and had serious doubts about whether it would ever open again. Some difficult and extreme measures had to be taken if we wanted this treasured place to continue. After two hard years, we are thrilled to find our café thriving. More than ever before.

From the beginning, the café was to be different from businesses whose main goal was to grow themselves. We wanted to be generous in all we did. Which almost ran us into the ground. Generosity is undoubtedly a goal we still hold, but we have come to define it in new ways, ways that I have found helpful for ministry on both an organizational and personal level.

The purpose of a business is to continue. It builds itself up for the purpose of continuing; it reinvests in itself for the purpose of sustaining itself and growing itself. It makes choices that will keep itself alive. This is good and normal for a business. But it seems inward focused compared to ministry.

Because a ministry exists to bless. And so in everything we do in ministry, we empty ourselves, give away more than we receive. Ask little in return. Which looks very outward focused, very selfless. And it is. Until we run ourselves out of business. And then what help are we to anyone?

So we made some changes. It meant we had to say no to anything that limited our ability to bless and continue to bless. Anything that kept people from feeling welcome had to go, including behaviors of other guests. Some regulars felt so at home in the café that it meant bringing their dogs inside. For one regular it meant clipping his toenails in the café! Those few people were so comfortable that they made many others uncomfortable. It threatened both our ability to welcome everyone and our ability to keep welcoming everyone (if we lost too many customers it would begin to affect our financial sustainability). So we had to say, "You are welcome. And your dog is welcome—on the porch" and "You are welcome. But your toenail clippers are not."

Around the same time some members of our church wanted to host a regular meal for homeless people. Our call to hospitality made it seem like a natural fit. But as we explored the health and safety issues involved, the time and energy that would be required of our staff, we had to say it wasn't possible for us. It felt wrong to say no to a ministry to the homeless, but if we were committed to our existing café ministry and continuing to bless people through it, we couldn't ask our café staff to both run a café and manage the new needs of a meal ministry.

If we believe it is good for us to be here, doing what we're doing (whether we're a Christian café, a church or an individual servant), isn't it an important part of our call not only to bless but to *continue* to bless? And so we're learning in our decision-making processes to bring this dual calling into play. We're learning to ask, "What will help us not only to continue and not only to bless, but to continue to bless?" In our ministry plans, rather than storing away resources only to protect our continuation or giving away resources only to empty ourselves, we look for ways to bless in a way that allows us to continue to bless year after year.

The business-ministry divide sometimes creates a false choice of selfishness versus selflessness. But when we understand that the best way to bless is to be here long-term, these issues stop being "our needs versus their needs" issues. If our ability to continue to be here means continuing to bless—even as we sustain ourselves as ministries, organizations and ministers—we do so for the sake of others.[6]

And so we find ourselves measuring bodies, buildings and budgets—but not as signs of success. We measure them as a way to make decisions about how we can continue to bless.[7] This feels like thriving, like living the abundant life. We give in a way that allows us to keep giving, year in and year out. We care for ourselves—as individual servants and as an organization—in a way that allows us to keep caring for others. This approach reframes our efforts to succeed. When we are driven to do well for the sake of others, it comes from a new place, a less competitive, ambitious place. We are no longer motivated by anxiety about meeting a quota or looking good to others but by a desire to keep doing good for others.

We've come to see that anxiety itself is a kind of diagnostic. Not because it's a problem to feel it—anxiety is a God-given response that makes us pay attention. The question is, will we lead from it? Anxiety can become a touchstone, an invitation not to engage but to disengage, at least for a while. If faithfulness means acting out of trust that we are in God's hands, anxiety can reveal to us when we're making decisions apart from faithfulness. This is not another excuse to go down the "Christians should never be anxious" road or to judge ourselves and each other. Neither is it an excuse to be passive or disengage permanently. But our anxiety is worth listening to, an opportunity to prayerfully decide how to engage well—from peace instead of self-preservation. What are we really worried about? Do we think God cares about it? If not, why are we worried about it? If so, why are we worried about it?

Practically speaking, no good idea has ever come to me when I've been anxious, but ideas have flowed when I've followed anxiety's invitation to step into rest and prayer. And almost all the dumb mistakes I've made have come from anxiety. In fact, it's a huge generalization, and there's no way I could ever prove it, but I have a theory that most of the human-made problems in the church (perhaps even in our world) come in some way from anxiety.

Reflect

Tell the story of anxiety in your work. What makes you anxious and how do you usually respond? What would it look like instead to lead from faithfulness?

If we truly believe that the same God who is in us is also in the world, this church and every believer, there must be a way forward— not always an easy way, but a way nonetheless. If we truly believe that his Word is truth and power, then we can set aside our striving in our own power to draw people to ourselves and see our part in God's work to draw all people to himself. This kind of faithfulness trusts that nothing is too challenging for God to overcome, that success may not come in our lifetime, that even if this particular congregation disappeared, the work of the kingdom would go on.

That kind of faithfulness is a lovely ideal, but how do we become and remain faithful? Is this just a new kind of pressure to put on ourselves? A new standard of performance? As vulnerable humans, there are limits to our ability to control and maintain our motivations. The answer to all these questions is uncomplicated in that it's one word. But once we begin to explore it in practice, it unfolds into the most beautiful, mysterious, ever-unfolding wonder: sabbath. We've touched on it already in the context of rest, but the longer I practice sabbath, the more I see what it means for work, even for notions of success. I have come to a place where I've discovered that, ironically, working well comes from learning how to *not* work.

It's a joke around UCC that I'm a strange boss because I'm always telling my staff to rest. When I'm checking in with them about how they're doing personally and how their ministries are going, any sign that something is in the way of thriving leads me to ask, "How are you resting?" I try to take my own advice too, and so it was on a recent retreat that I had time to reflect on why rest means so much for vulnerable humans who want to figure out faithfulness, success and thriving.

I found a tiny cabin by a river for this winter retreat. As soon as I arrived, I sat to undo my shoes—just for a minute, before I got on with my afternoon of "productive retreat activities." But the recliner would have none of that. So I settled in to warm myself from the chill. Soon my novel was conspiring with the recliner and I opened it to where I'd last left it: Anne Rice's telling of a young Jesus discovering his call. My half-sleeping, half-reading experience in that recliner became inextricable from Rice's description of Jesus escaping to his favorite olive grove:

> [The] layer of leaves had long covered [the stones] so that the place was soft there for lying, just as an open field might be with silken grass, and in its own way just as sweet. I had a roll of clean rags with me for a pillow. I crept in and lay down and allowed myself a long slow breath. I thanked the Lord for this enclosure, for this escape. I looked up at the play of light in the mesh of faintly moving branches. The winter days faded abruptly. The sky was already colorless. I didn't mind. . . . I prayed; I tried to clear my mind. It was fragrant and wholesome here.[8]

With him I breathed; I prayed. Jesus of all people should have had no time for such deep rest—the salvation of all humanity was on his shoulders. And yet the Gospel writers tell us about the times he found rest. Sweet rest.

As my eyes closed, my mind held the image of Jesus' olive grove, and I was the one sleeping at the foot of the ancient trees. In that place of rest God brought to mind memories of recent months in ministry, time to finally reflect back on all my mind and heart had carried but hadn't yet understood. He drew my attention to the branches above me, laden with beautiful fruit. He reminded me of the church's twenty-fifth anniversary, just the month before, when we had reflected on John 15 and celebrated many stories of the faithfulness of many followers over many years, many acts of selflessness, many lives restored, many hearts healed, many workers sent—much lasting fruit.

As I lay there in that recliner/olive grove, somehow it became a vineyard as well. Whether I was looking up at olives or grapes was unimportant. What was important was the energy I felt surging through this trunk, the life I saw bursting into fruit above me, the faces in each flourishing. I knew I had some part in the growth of this plant and yet here I was resting in the shade of it, celebrating the fruit and my small part in it. It certainly was an unpredictable plant but no longer in a way I resented. I smiled, wondering when I'd learned to enjoy the thrill and mystery of tending a plant beyond my control.

But there were disturbing memories still to be processed from the year past, and from the safety of my recliner/olive grove I felt ready to reflect on the many acts of terrorism and violence we'd watched around the world. I had just read a CNN article that began with the words "Even terrorists have fears," which struck me as strange.[9] As far as I could see, fear is *all* a terrorist has. It's why he feels the need to protect his interests in violent ways. Those of us who aren't terrorists may not take up bombs, but we have our own arsenals. Fears become self-fulfilling when they drive us to behave in desperate ways that bring opposition and suffering. We may not bring physical harm, but we harm hearts and relationships when we force our ways on each other, impose our programs and agendas out of fear that we won't be successful. We become like terrorists, doubtful that there is goodness or safety for us, forcing responses from others that only confirm our fears and increase them. We create scarcity by living according to scarcity.

Here I thought back on a book I'd read that year—*Slow Church*—that connects the work of farming to the work of pastoring. There is a kind of terrorism that applies to agriculture when we don't trust that the soil is good, that the seed knows what to do, that the rain will come, but resort to chemicals and technology to wring productivity from the ground.[10] What would it look like to study the soil and discover what it wants to grow? To respond to what is thriving? How can we live out a deep peace that there is goodness, provision, God? When we sense our inability to control all the factors that contribute to our view of success, when we don't have the answers, when we can't fix people or social ills, when folks leave the church, when we don't all agree and we realize how little we control, will we get desperate, turn to a kind of terrorism? Or will we see these challenges as a way to true success, an invitation to know our limits and trust in greater forces?

I had no answers to those questions, but I was ready to think about something else. God then drew my attention to the week I had just finished. I had finally found what all preachers long for: a new take on the Christmas story! In all my previous readings, I'd never before noticed the poetic lines that end Zechariah's song:

> By the tender mercy of our God,
>   the dawn from on high will break upon us,
> to give light to those who sit in darkness and in the shadow of
>   death,
>   to guide our feet into the way of peace. (Luke 1:78-79 NRSV)

When I had come across this passage in preparation for the Christmas Eve homily, each word had washed over me with its warm promises. I never use the word *balm*, but it was the first that came to mind. In this, the busiest time of year, I had been called to remember that it was *his* tender mercy, *his* dawn breaking from on high, *his* gift of light, *his* guidance. Here under these verdant branches in this wintry cabin God was drawing my attention back to those words I spoke at Christmas, reminding me that our role is to receive the light, to let ourselves be led in the way of peace. And that is peace—to know what is our part and what is his. From that rest comes much fruit—fruit that lasts.

Reflect

What appeals to you about the image of resting against the roots of a tree and looking up at the fruit? What fruit that lasts would you count as you look up?

Even though that recliner eventually released me again to the world, the memory of the roots against my shoulder remained with me. Even as I returned to work, as I studied and led meetings and taught and wrote emails, I knew my spirit was still lying in that orchard. I knew there was a way to abide and bear fruit at the same time. If every electric impulse that gives my heart a beat, every neural twitch that shapes a thought, every gift of breath that allows me to do this work is from him, my work is his. If every member of the community is filled with the same Spirit at work in me, my work is his.

So as I live in this orchard/vineyard, resting and working all at once, I'm starting to understand why Jesus used so many agricultural metaphors—raising plants means work but also partnership and trust. I've never had a successful garden, but everything I know about gardening I've learned from ministry. And in ministry we hope for results: growth and fruit are good; they're signs of life; they cannot be faked. While Jesus wasn't concerned about buildings, bodies and budgets, he did talk a lot about fruit.[11]

In ministry we don't measure health or fruit or thriving in statistics. We're intimately engaged with our garden, watching everywhere for human hearts that are turning to God. Seeing signs that love, joy, peace, forbearance, kindness, goodness, faithfulness, gentleness and self-control are growing. Noticing where people are discovering passions and using gifts, where hearts are learning both to receive God's care and to care about what he cares about. Giving nourishment in those places. And as we look for signs of health and growth, we are surprised by what we did not plant. We learn to have peace with what is in our hands and what is not. We certainly work hard but with a deep appreciation that the seed, the ground, the rain, the sun, even the worms are out of our control. This peace teaches who God is—and that it's not us.

When we embrace our true identity in him and set aside our efforts to be him, it fills us more than any of our own efforts could. We learn a strange kind of confidence in knowing our place, trusting that God can work in and through and because of and in spite of us. If all is in his hands, what have we to fear? If this church is his church, what does our stressful striving accomplish? If he can bring goodness and lessons from failure and pain, even life from death, where is the victory of anything that seems to overcome us?

From that peace we are able to be deeply, wholly, truly present. Having learned who God is and who we are, we admit our efforts to prove something or gain approval, and so we set aside our preoccupation with self—how this work makes us feel, how it makes us look—and turn with real attentiveness to the life around us. With our heart, mind, spirit and all our senses we watch and tend. We learn seasons and signs of unhealth; we rise every morning to take note of what has bloomed overnight, what is withering. And we know how to respond.

Gardening requires peace and presence. So does faithful ministry led by limited, vulnerable people. These are habits that take a lifetime to learn. And there's nothing like sabbath to teach them to us. Once we put sabbath on our weekly calendar, it wants to become a part of our days and our hours and our minutes. A weekly practice is a good way to start, but it soon leaks over into our whole life.

The traditional Jewish celebration of sabbath ends with a meal. In this havdalah meal, participants take part in several multisensory metaphors that remind them of both the separateness of sabbath and the way all the other days of the week are sanctified by sabbath. Wine is poured into a cup until it overflows, symbolizing how the blessings of sabbath overflow into the rest of life. As we embrace sabbath practice, even if it begins with a lunch break, we will begin to see how it becomes abundance. The rest we receive from sabbath will overflow into our work. The identity we embrace from sabbath will overflow into our work. The peace we learn from sabbath will overflow into our work. Not a peace without conflict but a peace that sees God able to work in all things, even the conflict, a peace that trusts God can use us, even our failures. This is a peace that he works in ways we can't see, that he provides our needs, that he longs even more than we do for our hearts and communities to thrive. This is a peace in the fullness of God's presence.

Sabbath helps us be faithful in our personal walk and prayer life because it teaches us that kind of peace and presence. Sabbath helps us be faithful in our reading of the Bible, bringing our whole selves and laying down our "weapons." Sabbath helps us successfully shape culture, develop leaders, use our time and energy, because it teaches us to be present and peaceful in the mess of daily life with people. Sabbath helps us as the people of God to be present and peaceful in the way we engage with the world.

My sense of whether it was a "successful" day cannot be about whether I had amazing results, impressed a lot of people or knew all the answers. If it were, I would never have a successful day. My sense of whether the church I lead is successful cannot only be about how much we all agree or we would never have success. At the end of the day, I know whether my staff and I have been faithful based on whether we were present and peaceful. And I know whether my church is a "success" based on whether its engagement with the community is present and peaceful. How are we at peace that God is at work in and through and because of and in spite of us? How are we wholly present in our community, trusting that he is also present?

Reflect

How can you move toward peace and faithfulness through practices of rest? What would it look like to cease operating from anxiety?

PART THREE

PRACTICING IN PUBLIC

Vulnerability with an Audience

11

Welcome to the Process

How Vulnerable Pastors Teach and Preach

Herding sheep isn't easy. As pastors, we imagine that if we just tell people stuff—the right stuff, enough stuff—we'll fix their relationships, answer their questions, get them into the category "saved" or "mature" or even "small group leader." We might even reach that point where everyone finally gets it.

Yes, it's a pipe dream to expect all our congregants to arrive, but every pastor at some point feels frustration like: *How can this couple's marriage be falling apart? We just talked about this issue in a sermon series!* Or, *How can this individual be walking away from faith? I just did a Bible study with her last month!* There can't be many jobs more frustrating than facilitating human learning and growth. We're tempted to give people a list of tasks or doctrines so that once they've checked off that list, we can check them off our list. But before we talk about how we teach, let's think about how we learn.

Like most Christian organizations, UCC has core values, core beliefs and a mission statement. We're also beginning to name our core practices. In the end, what we're doing as individuals and as a community is stepping into a never-ending process of growth, living into truths we will never see fully realized. As we live into them we come to believe them more and more.

Some of the deepest and most lasting growth I've seen in my own life and the life of others has come from one question: "If I really believed *x*, how would I live differently?" One couple said, "If we really believed God loved us regardless of what we accomplished, we'd be more willing to rest." As uncomfortable as it made them, they stepped into rest and began to trust in God's delight in them. Another individual said, "If I really believed God loved and invited me, I'd be more willing to invite people into my home, even when it's a mess." So she started offering impromptu invitations and, in them, trusting more in God's love in the mess. Another family said, "If we really believed in God's abundance, we would give more." And in giving from their scarcity they are learning to believe in abundance.

> Jesus said, "If you want to know the truth of what I'm saying, you have to do what I say." There's no guarantee that the authoritative word is going to make any sense to you unless you do what it says.
>
> **Esther Lightcap Meek**[1]

We hold many beliefs in this life that we will never see in their fullness. We believe God is good and yet this world is broken. We believe God is generous and yet we know lack. We believe in resurrection and yet everything is touched with death and decay. We are living two truths, but we know one of them is the truer and so we step into it. It's hard to live against the truth of this world, so we need a community of others stepping into it with us and reminding us every day that we are not alone or delusional. This allows us as a community to reveal the love and abundance of God to the world, to live into a new creation now—at least in part.[2] Our communities can become places where the greater truth reigns—through selflessness, generosity, hopefulness and hospitality—even imperfectly. Our practices express who we are, all the while forming us to be more who we are.

CORE PRACTICES

Our church community has decided to watch and embrace the practices that help us to live into our beliefs. It's a work in progress (which seems fitting) but so far this is our list of core practices.

Ritual and rhythm of life. This means "continually devoting ourselves" as a community, as families and as individuals to simple daily faithfulness shaped by Scripture, prayer, Communion and sabbath keeping, whether we're feeling it or not.

Process and tension. We are committed to the truth that spiritual growth and sanctification are lifelong processes without quick fixes or easy answers and that the tension of longing for truths we don't yet see is a process that itself shapes us.

Generosity. We desire to speak and live gratefully (even if we don't feel grateful, even if it means sacrifice or comes during suffering), expressing this through generosity with money but also with time, gifts, resources.

Hospitality. We ask, "How does our Sunday worship, our use of our homes, our building, our lives express the welcome we have received from Christ?"

Patience. This is an ongoing commitment to mission with humble acceptance that we may not always see the fruit, trusting that it is God who works in hearts and adds to our number.

These practices have grown out of the description of early Christian community in Acts 2.[3] And they're an ongoing investigation of the fascination I have with Lauren Winner's words:

> Practice is to Judaism what belief is to Christianity. That is not to say that Judaism doesn't have dogma or doctrine. It is rather to say that for Jews, the essence of the thing is a doing, an action. Your faith might come and go, but your practice ought not waver. (Indeed, Judaism suggests that the repeating of the practice is the best way to ensure that a doubter's faith will return.)[4]

Reflect

What core practices shape your community? How can you acknowledge them as part of the community's learning process?

If we see spiritual development unfolding in this humble commitment to process, it will naturally influence us to see ourselves as facilitators of that development in the lives of others. Teaching and preaching will come to be less "one and done" and more an interweaving of truth with the daily life and practices of the community. Our words on Sundays become part of an ongoing conversation with lived realities, an engagement with small group discussions and dinner table arguments and personal ruminations. As we watch how our words interact with life, we're humbled to see how one member hears the same idea for years but never applies it and inspired to see how another member takes our words and comes to know them more deeply than we ever did.

> The body is a specially marked off preserve, a repository of ultimate value. The human body does not merely front for or point to the sacred; it is sacred, a locus of revelation.... Not only does skin "think" ... skin "reveals." ... Ritual knowledge is gained by and through the body.
> **Ronald Grimes[5]**

When I first preached about Jesus' Gethsemane prayer as a model prayer (see chapter 7), I didn't see its potential. When I said, "I don't know what God *will* do, but I know what he *can* do," I was simply summing up Jesus' prayer. It wasn't until I watched others exploring this comment that I saw what it held. When Jennifer and Jason first came to UCC, I recognized the signs of pastor burnout. They had planted a church that had crumbled after only a year and suddenly they were without a job, a church community, a sense of mission. And they had a lot of questions for God. This simple statement, contrasting what God will do and can do, resonated with them. Jennifer's exploration of it became a song:

Lord, we lift our sister, lift her to you
She's paralyzed by grievous wounds.
Don't leave her here, we beg of you
For by faith we know what you can do.
Lord our brother's tired, see him bowed down
For lies he's known have left him bound.
We're on our knees beside him now
Asking for deliverance somehow.
We don't know what
And we don't know when
but we know that you are good.
No eye has seen
No ear has heard
The plans you have for us
So we surrender to your love.

When I heard Jen sing this song, I recognized a seed of my idea but she had allowed it to grow into something beautiful. This couple had taken an idea and wrestled with it through time and tears and discovered something new.

Reflect

How have you watched people in your community take your ideas and run with them? How could you encourage that even more?

Teaching for that kind of discovery invites us into a process that we as teachers also personally engage in—we as a community join in it together. We preachers are often careful to end our sermons with application points so that our sermons don't remain in the clouds. But we can be so prescriptive that we run down the bullet points and move on to announcements without allowing for true engagement. We open up a vista of possibilities and then, just when our people are awed by the scope of something new, we shut it down with action steps.

"Since we're talking about giving, why not give to this missionary we support?"

"Since we're talking about service, we've got a children's festival next week, so look for the sign-up sheet in the foyer."

Of course, action is what we want, but do our sermons ask the question and answer it before our listeners have a chance to hang in the in-between? Learning can be uncomfortable: questioning old ideas, challenging cozy habits. It's not our job as teachers to help people avoid the discomfort but to create space for them to pay attention and learn from it. Instead of serving up prepackaged applications, perhaps we could see our sermons as a field trip that collects people from where they live, takes them to a broad, open place and says, "Go explore and let's meet back here so that on the way home we can talk about what we've found."

Application can mean simply asking people to engage in the same old practices but with new watchfulness. Often my associate pastor Anthony shares this application: "Keep being in Scripture, prayer and Christian community and trust that it is shaping you." He is known for talking "tension" as much as I'm known for talking "process." Whatever we call it, it's good for learners to have permission to learn, to try, to fail, to try again. Whatever energy we once put into anxiety about not having arrived we can now invest in the journey.

Reflect

What would it look like for your teaching to give permission to be in process?

This invitation to explore can take the form of post-sermon testimonies. When we invite people at UCC to share testimonies as an application of the sermon, I start by asking my colleagues for suggestions of people who are learning the lessons of the sermon, and together we choose a diverse group. I help those giving testimonies to shape their story (which is a leadership development opportunity in itself), providing clear direction about what we would like them to share and for how long and at what point in the service. I suggest that they put their story in writing and offer to pray with them. I'm always sure to say, "Don't only tell how you've arrived; share what you're still figuring out," and "Don't just talk ideas. Tell a story." It's beautiful to watch how those who share testimonies often get the "Your words meant so much to me" feedback after the service.

On the other hand, application may mean shaping a question for listeners to process with their small groups and families. For one series we handed out miniature journals and posted a question each week (through email, Facebook and the bulletin) to invite reflection and conversation. We made time for the question to be explored during the service, through personal journaling or quiet reflection time. When people give us an hour of their week, it's a gift to give a little of it back to them in the form of silence.

Other times we invite the community to process together: one day the sermon extended the Ecclesiastes metaphor of chasing after wind by talking about flying a kite, living more lightly with the fleeting things of life. During the worship set we invited people (things like this are always optional) to move forward, take a tiny origami kite and write on it something they wanted to live with more lightly ("body image," "work," "romantic expectations"), then string it up so that all our colorful kites fluttered over our heads. The fluttering itself captured the freedom of that day's learning and we saw how we were learning together.

Another day the public sharing of applications took a different turn. To explore resurrection, we asked, "What feels like death?" As we shuffled forward to take Communion, each person had a chance (again, always optional) to write their answer on a large chalkboard ("depression," "injustice," "divorce") as a way to hope for resurrection in that place. Sharing our own applications is a kind of tiny testimony. Seeing the applications of others alongside ours reminds us we're part of a community in process.

Liturgical elements can encourage the discovery of application. Taking Communion can be a place of application, especially if the point is receiving forgiveness or embracing community. Responsive readings (or singings) offer practical steps forward. And prayer is a way to explore application. If the sermon was about engaging with the world, our guided prayer after the sermon can relate the concept to life: "Father, each of us has gifts and opportunities to engage in this world. We bring to mind the ways we spend our days. Show us how to use them for you. (Pause.) We bring to mind the people we see in our communities. Show us how to share your love with them. (Pause.)"

However we chose to do it, this ending with an invitation to explore adds vitality to the community as the scriptural truth takes on different textures everywhere it is applied. If we prepare the hoped-for outcome in advance, to be served up at the end of the teaching, we run the risk of creating a one-size-fits-all application that actually fits no one. We potentially rob learners of the opportunity to explore how God wants to apply the teaching in their jobs, homes, personalities. But as members of the community have a conversation with God and each other, the application takes on the fullness of the multicolored, multifaceted, multigifted body of Christ. This practice and process becomes a way to heal the damage done by modernity and the industrial revolution: the focus on product and on humans as producers, the body-spirit divide, the loss of the identity that we once found in tradition and ritual. And we are whole and human again.

Reflect

What does application usually look like in your teaching and preaching? How could you invite those you teach to be part of naming the application?

For our teaching to truly welcome a community into the process, we as teachers have to be willing to welcome a community into *our* process. This idea actually makes my stomach turn. Being in process is hard enough, even harder in front of people and on a regular basis. Whatever part of me stresses over performance joins with whatever is an introverted perfectionist and hunkers down in cornered desperation at the prospect. So I justify my hesitation with words like Henri Nouwen's: "This does not mean that ministers or priests must, explicitly, bring their own sins or failures into the pulpit or into their daily ministries. That would be unhealthy and imprudent and not at all a form of servant leadership." Of course it wouldn't be right for me to share my weaknesses!

Which works right up until I read his next sentence: "What it means is that ministers . . . are also called to be full members of their communities, are accountable to them and need their affection and support, and are called to minister with their whole being, including their wounded selves."[6] I've yet to figure out that perfect balance of sharing personal struggles in a healthy way in my teaching. All I can do is keep asking myself, "Whose interests are you really protecting here?" And then asking myself again with a reminder to be honest this time.

Given that we each have different personalities and settings, there's no formula for healthy vulnerability in preaching and teaching. But the final word is: what is right can't be based on what feels right but on what is both good for our people and true to God's work in our lives. We may never arrive at a policy on vulnerability for every situation, and that's part of our vulnerability—to figure it out as we go and give ourselves grace when we over- or undershare. Here are questions I ask to discern healthy vulnerability in teaching:

- What kind of vulnerability am I comfortable or uncomfortable with? Why?

- What am I afraid of? Who am I trying to emulate or impress?

- Am I sharing to draw attention to myself in a prideful way? Am I keeping God's work in my life to myself in a prideful way?

- Am I letting the culture cloud my judgment (especially as it relates to gender and social norms)? How does my family experience influence what feels right?

- If I really believe my authority and identity are from God, my success and failures are God's, will I share differently? How can I move toward that even if it's uncomfortable?

- How can I share in a way that people are left with the memory of God's work, not mine?

Discerning all of that takes me back to God, asks him to reveal my unspoken motivations, helps me become familiar with that excruciating vulnerability before him, teaches me how to step into it with others.

My anxiety about revealing my true, in-process self is why till my dying day I will remember my valedictory speech. When you're valedictorian, people expect something remarkable. Luckily, I was exempted from final exams to prepare. And by the time convocation rolled around, I had finely tuned a manuscript and memorized every word. As the last chord of the final hymn died out, all I had to do was approach the podium, lift my head and press "play." After graduation, my ministry took the form of freelance writing and guest speaking. So I worked away undisturbed in my home, polishing pearls for publishers and event planners. Some weeks the writing was threatened by a personal issue, but for the most part I was free to shape my ideas until they shone.

When I became a pastor I knew I had a lot to learn about sermon prep. What skills allow a pastor to fully develop a sermon every week while handling not only her own family and personal stuff but also the family and personal stuff of a whole congregation? How could I find that untouched, creative place for pearl polishing? So I slaved away, managing the distractions of pastoral duties to protect a place to replicate that valedictory speech. And every Sunday after preaching I stepped down from the pulpit feeling flat.

I thought it was my job to create a beautiful product, divorced from the messiness of life. But preaching forces me to become part of the product, always in the mess—my own and others'. Instead of imparting otherworldly enlightenment to me in my quiet study, God seeks embodiment, wants to use my life as the testing ground for each sermon. If I expect each individual in the congregation to find some connection between life and text that week, why shouldn't I expect the same of myself?

Which makes me look differently at my congregation: how can their weekly needs for encouragement, prayer and discipleship be a distraction from sermon preparation when they can provide new ways to watch how the Word collides with life? My need for God and their need for God and our need for each other become inseparable. I'm less ashamed of the subjectivity of my stories. While storytelling does not always feel safe, it's worth the risk because "the power of storytelling goes beyond the border of the story itself. It moves into the nooks and crannies of our memories and emotions, sometimes gently, sometimes explosively, revealing, awakening, shocking, calling."[7]

And so my preparation to teach or preach begins with a willingness to let Scripture into my own story. I often begin by laying myself down—literally. Lying down and listening to Scripture reminds me that while I have work to do in the teaching of this community, the work is not mine to do on others. The work is God's to perform in us—starting with me. And so I lie in bed and listen to the passage over and over, taking note of where it brings tears, annoyance or comfort. The places it snags on my heart hint at the potential the passage has in the hearts of others. I trust that my congregation and I are learning together; I just get a preview. But the preview doesn't mean I'm finished learning by Sunday, so I have to take the advice I give to those sharing testimonies: "Don't only tell how you've arrived; share what you're still figuring out." And "Don't just talk ideas. Tell a story."

As I think back on that valedictory speech, I remember a fullness of confidence and bright lights shielding a dark audience. I remember holding out a tiny, hard, perfectly polished pearl at arm's length for all to see. "Look what I made!" But when I think about my sermons, I recognize a gnawing inadequacy to find words big enough to express the miraculous things I'm still learning. I think about faces. Faces napping occasionally. But mostly faces smiling, nodding, focused, contemplative, tearful. Faces I've been with all week, whose stories I know. I have come to recognize that moment when someone is still looking at me but they're no longer seeing me. On my insecure days it's disappointing to feel I've lost them, but on my good days I see they've been found.

And somehow, some days even I feel found. These are the days when nothing has gone right and by Sunday morning I have little to bring—but I have no choice but to stand up and say something. While the idea of holding out a polished pearl is very appealing, God keeps telling me, "You're the pearl I'm polishing" and holding me out for all to see. I don't usually feel particularly pearl-like and certainly not polished. By the time I return to my seat I often feel flat, so it makes no worldly sense to hear someone say, "That was powerful!"

I want to respond, "I was shaking up there. I can hardly remember what I said. You think it was powerful? Who were you listening to?" But I know there's a difference between how I feel in delivering a sermon and what God can do in the heart of a hearer (which is also evident on the days I feel great about my performance). So if I know God works in the gaps, I need to be better at leaving them.

One Sunday God let me watch this lesson in the life of someone else. I had asked Jenna to read a psalm. When she arrived before the service, I could see something wasn't right. She and her husband were in the final throes of a major move and the emotional upheaval of it had hit her that morning, leading to a hurtful pre-church blowup with her husband. As a professional performer, she knew how to pull herself together. As a professional performer, she skipped the option I gave her to let someone else do the reading. She would suck it up. The show must go on. When she agreed to go ahead with the reading, these were my words to her (well-rehearsed from using them on myself): "You can choose to see your emotional state as a distraction, something to get in the way of your performance, or as fuel for a reading that is truly present."

It was beautiful to see how she chose the latter. It helped that the assigned reading was Psalm 69. She could say, "I am worn out calling for help; my throat is parched" with real angst. She could voice, "Come near and rescue me!" with believable longing. We didn't leave impressed with Jenna's dramatic reading. Instead, her honest expression of emotion left us with the impression of a human engaging in a real way with God. It gave us permission to do the same. It made an ancient psalm vital and fresh. It presented the possibility that just because she, and we, feel forsaken by God, it does not mean we are. In watching her, I watched my own struggle to share the process and decided again to press myself into it. Even when I have very little to share.

I'm sure I'm not the only preacher who feels inadequate while preparing sermons. Almost every week I think, *Will this be the week when I have nothing to say?* Ideas rarely flow as easily as we pastors would like. Texts refuse to make sense. Life gets in the way. Even when we have a great vision, our words seem pale. I've often used the metaphor of holding a few crumbs, feeling like I have little to offer a hungry crowd. The shame of that paucity has made me want to clench my fist tight, even resent the crowd for wanting more than I have to give. But over time I've found a friend in the little boy with the loaves and fish. Although it was obviously not enough, he gave what he had and we know how God used it. So every week I look at my hands, see the crumbs and ask God to make my measly offering enough.

These prayers have broadened my perspective, and yet recently I saw how limiting they can be.

The last time I prayed this crumb prayer, the idea of feeding a multitude reminded me of myself as a young wife. Whenever we used to invite guests for dinner, I spent the entire day working myself into a frenzy so that by the time the guests arrived, every garnish was in place, every surface shone—and I just wanted to go to bed. I'd then spend the evening worrying if my guests noticed the chicken was dry and that I'd missed a smudge on the windows. I wonder if my guests spent the evening feeling sorry for the trouble they were causing me and were glad when the evening was over. After many years I've learned to keep the planning simple, and on my best days I pray for the guests while I'm chopping vegetables or take a nap to be sure I'm genuine in my welcome by the time the doorbell rings. The focus is not on the food or house but on the time together.

I'm just beginning to explore what it means to bring those hospitality lessons into my preaching. After all, when I preach, I'm inviting people to share an experience. The preparation is necessary—cleaning and cooking in the case of entertaining, study and writing in the case of preaching—but does it have to be the only focus? Christian hospitality over the years has welcomed believers and non-believers alike to experience the love of God. Couldn't my approach to preaching also welcome them in? Will my prayers be for myself to be ready and for my sermon to be well-shaped? Or will my prayers be for those who come?

When preparing for guests at home, I don't pray for the food but for the ones who will eat it. The crumb prayer has me looking down at my own hand. A hospitable approach, while still conscious that I have only crumbs, lifts my head to the hungry mass. As I think of their needs instead of my fears, I'm able to see them. The more I get over myself and focus on the needs of my guests, the more they'll leave feeling blessed. The less they'll notice my little stammers and hesitations, the times I lost my place and had to check my notes. The more they'll experience the welcome of God. This is our task as preachers and teachers, not to give quick resolutions and easy answers that end the quest but to extend welcome.

Our sermons say, "Welcome into ongoing nourishment and growth."

"Welcome into dialogue with God and a learning community."

"Welcome into mystery."

"Welcome into relationship."

"Welcome into adventure."

"Welcome to the process."

Exercises for
Vulnerable Teaching and Preaching

- Set yourself a challenge to preach on passages or topics that make you uncomfortable, admitting to your congregation what you don't like or understand and how you wrestle with that.
- Invite others into the process of preparation. Ask select laypeople or coworkers to process ideas with you, share their thoughts and give feedback before and after the sermon.

- Take note of when you include your own stories: are they funny illustrations to work toward your main point or stories of how you're applying the main point? Share how you're learning the lesson, including how you're messing up. Use present tense ("I'm learning that . . . " or "We're growing in . . . ") rather than past ("I learned" or "We grew") to communicate the ongoing process of personal and community growth.
- When you refer to yourself, use self-effacing language (without leaning toward self-hatred). If you must tell a story of a negative example, use yourself but with patience for your own learning. To give a positive example, find someone else. When you make a mistake in a sermon (however you define that), don't take yourself too seriously. The grace you give yourself will give grace to others.

12

The Right Kind of Desperate

How Vulnerable Pastors Engage with the World

W e've confessed our human vulnerabilities and begun to see opportunities for God to show his power in our personal faith, prayer and Bible study, in our church culture and rhythms of life, in our leading and teaching. So now, what can vulnerability bring to the way we reach outside of the church, often into hostile territory? How will renewed vision of our limitations redefine the work of the kingdom and reveal our solidarity with the lost and broken?

I don't often use the word *kingdom*. I avoid it because it sounds like colonization. When I hear Christians talk about kingdom, it often turns to talk about buildings and staff and logos and websites and marketing campaigns. If that's what it takes, I don't know the first thing about making the kingdom. And we know enough history for the word *kingdom* to bring to mind despotic rulers, useless aristocrats and power-hungry feudal lords.

> Christianity not only injected some of its DNA into empire (thus Christianizing it), but empire has injected its DNA into Christianity, thus imperializing our Christianity. It is nearly impossible to understand how deep the infection goes.
>
> **Mark Van Steenwyk**[1]

Kingdom makes us think of physical things—walls, armies, weapons— things that seem solid, strong. But every manmade thing that seems invincible eventually falls to ruin.

For generations Israel longed to be a kingdom—as nomadic shepherds, as slaves in Egypt, as desert wanderers. Finally in their own land they had judges and prophets but begged God for a king like the other nations had. And the kings they'd always wanted turned out, like all kings, to be flawed human beings. Eventually, in exile, Israel had to live under the rule of foreign kings. Throughout that history they waited for the one who would lead them. When Jesus came they were living under Roman rule with a king put in place by Rome.

The Israelite people have, from the beginning of their story, been longing for the security and identity of a king. But throughout their story God has yearned for them to find their identity and security in him. This is why Jesus talks so much about God's kingdom, to reveal it in a new way.

> He told them another parable: "The kingdom of heaven is like a mustard seed, which a man took and planted in his field. Though it is the smallest of all seeds, yet when it grows, it is the largest of garden plants and becomes a tree, so that the birds come and perch in its branches."
>
> He told them still another parable: "The kingdom of heaven is like yeast that a woman took and mixed into about sixty pounds of flour until it worked all through the dough." (Matthew 13:31-33)

As Christians at the center of the world's power, we also need to see kingdom in a new way. One of the best things I've read about the kingdom of God has nothing to do with the kingdom of God. It's about toast. Well, at least it starts there. The article tells the story of the rising popularity of toast among hipsters in San Francisco, and the author admits to rolling his eyes that another ordinary thing has become artisanal and overpriced.[2] He decides to trace its roots, expecting that this latest coffee shop trend might find its genesis in some marketing office. But the story takes him somewhere unexpected.

After visiting three coffee houses, the author is directed to Trouble Coffee and Coconut Club, where he meets the owner, Giulietta Carrelli. And here's where the story becomes about much more than toast. Giulietta has a condition called schizo-affective disorder, which combines symptoms of schizophrenia and bipolarity. Sometimes she's gregarious and fun and other times she has what she calls "trouble"— psychotic episodes that throughout her adult life have left her homeless and unable to maintain close relationships. Such a pendulum-swing life leaves her disoriented and insecure, searching for something that feels dependable.

For Giulietta cinnamon toast is comfort food. And so instead of serving what's cool in her coffee shop, she shares what's meaningful to her. Not in an effort to start a trend but because toast has comforted her and she knows that everyone needs comfort. She's giving comfort and strength to others out of what has given her comfort and strength. And it's taken off, not only in her little café but across San Francisco and eventually in other urban areas across the United States.

When we want to start a kingdom trend, where do we start? Are we willing to begin by looking within and seeing our need for security and identity—our need for a king? It takes courage to trust that our own questions and yearnings are connected to the questions and yearnings of all human beings. It feels small, like a mustard seed, like a little yeast. Mustard seeds die to become trees; yeast is invisible once it's kneaded in. We may never understand how kingdom things happen or who starts them. But we know they are most powerful when they begin with a broken person who feels untethered and looks to the king for comfort or strength. What they find in him is so transforming that it takes root, grows in them into something they have to share. It drives them to serve, to talk about it, to help others find it. They may not even know they've been part of a movement. Whatever change we bring to the world can begin with how we've been changed.

Reflect

How are the lost and broken seeking security and identity in your community? How can your reliance on God for security and identity help you connect with their needs?

This lesson unfolded for me over several years, through five seemingly unrelated experiences. These stories have connected my personal experience to what I see happening in the world. They imply that our own hunger holds clues for how the world hungers.

Four summers ago we stayed in a cabin on the Georgian Bay in Ontario. It was on a tiny island with only one other cabin. There were no roads, electricity, phones or running water; it was the kind of place where someone has to ferry you out to the island. When they drop you off, you say, "See you next week!" and hope you've brought enough stuff to last till then.

One afternoon I sat on the dock reading while my daughter swam in the lake. She was twelve and a fairly confident swimmer, but I still felt the need to look up occasionally to check on her as she swam from our island to the next. Soon I was so drawn into my book that I lost track of time. When I looked up I saw not one sign of movement on the surface of that whole great lake. She was not on the other island and there was no sign of her where I'd last seen her.

My mind grasped for solutions, leaping at first to the impulse to jump in. But as I looked at that flat blue surface to choose where to dive, I had no clue where to even start. My small arms and legs could not get me far before it was too late for her. When my own strength failed me, my mind flew to the phone, usually at my side to solve every problem. But I didn't have it—and who would I call anyway? There were no emergency services for miles. When technology failed me I thought to just yell for help, then remembered that my husband and son were on a fishing trip and there was no other human being for miles. After cycling through all the usual things I look to for comfort and help—my own ability, public services, technology, community—I finally faced the reality that the best thing I could do was get in a canoe, paddle to the other side of the island, and hope that the people in that cabin had a phone to call the mainland for help, at which point they would send someone out by boat. By then it would be beyond too late.

So I just filled my small lungs with air and let out the biggest sound I could make, which disappeared into the northern expanses. In this moment of parental panic, the very best I could do was cry her name:

"Zoë!"

"Zoë!"

"Zoë!"

There was no answer. Not a splash or a ripple. Finally, when my heart had almost given way, I heard a little noise at the end of the dock. And there she was! Just feet away, beside the very dock I stood on but out of eyesight and unable to hear me because her ears were underwater. As you can imagine, the relief hit me like pure joy and I swear I'd never felt so light. My tensed muscles relaxed, the adrenaline in my feet leaked away, my stomach knot released.

But late that night as I lay in bed reflecting on the day, the sense of my own inadequacy haunted me. All the things that make me feel strong and capable are not mine at all. They're wealth, privilege, technology, connection. The sense of absolute lack remained with me, along with the memory of crying out into the open space. Although nobody drowned that day, I remember sinking, sinking and desperately clambering for something secure to cling to.

Reflect

How are you becoming aware of your sinking?

Not long after our Canada vacation I watched a viral online video that showed I'm not the only one with that sinking feeling. Others are beginning to see how wealth, technology and developed culture prop us up and mask our own lack. In the video, comedian Louis CK tells Conan O'Brien about a time when a Bruce Springsteen song came on the radio while he was driving.[3] The song's soulful wails took him back to all the angst of high school, and as he felt his emotions rising he found himself reaching for his phone, hoping to distract himself from the loneliness. At this point the audience is laughing, but it's a nervous laugh. They know what he's talking about but they don't want to go there. They came to watch Conan as a way to avoid going there. But Louis goes there. And he takes the audience with him. Continuing his story, he says that instead of getting on his phone to dull the pain, he chose to pull over to the side of the road and weep, letting the sadness hit him like a truck. (More uncomfortable laughter.) He says, "Underneath everything in your life there's that forever empty."

In that moment this flippant comedian becomes a prophet, with his finger on the pulse of a numbed, overstimulated culture. I began to see that maybe we're all feeling that forever empty. Some are willing to talk about it but most are doing all we can to mask it. After my lakeside experience and this online moment with a comedian, I started to wonder if others, inside and outside of the church, were also feeling the sinking feeling.

Reflect

How do you see others, even people who wouldn't call themselves Christians, becoming aware of their sinking?

Which brings me to Holy Week. The Wednesday before Easter every year I attend a Catholic Tenebrae service that tells the story of the passion up to the moment of Jesus' death. In evangelical traditions, Easter Sunday can feel like "Jesus-died-but-then-he-rose-again-yay!" So I love to take time to let the Holy Week story unfold piece by piece. "Tenebrae" means darkness, and the service begins with a fully lit candelabra that, candle by candle, is gradually extinguished throughout the service. By the end the congregation is in darkness, and people leave in silence. The entire service is one of being willing to "go there," all lamentations and psalms of longing, voicing the desperation of the generations who have cried out to God for salvation. One of the readings is from Psalm 69:

> I am worn out with crying,
> with longing for my God.
> Rescue me from sinking in the mud;
> save me from my foes.
> Save me from the waters of the deep
> lest the waves overwhelm me.
> Do not let the deep engulf me
> nor death close its mouth on me.
> Lord, answer, for your love is kind;
> in your compassion, turn towards me.
> Do not hide your face from your servant;
> answer quickly for I am in distress.[4]

I had read along with this reading every year but I had never before *felt* along with it. My memory of my own "drowning" on that lakeshore remained with me. My desperate cries resonated with the longing of the world throughout the ages, crying out for a Savior to rescue us from the sinking, crying out for something to fill that forever empty. This was no longer the cries of a mother on the shore of a lake or the torment of a comedian on the side of the road; this was all humanity over the ages. And this was no longer just a need for help in a crisis or comfort in loneliness but a deep need for salvation.

Reflect

How has the church through history expressed a posture of crying out? How have we forgotten it?

Which brings me to the next story. I was honored to join a conversation of church leaders to dream about the future of the church. One session was devoted to discussing the most pressing issues facing us today: How to respond to injustices? How to give a voice to the oppressed? How to handle all the questions around sexuality? It was a heavy session, and as we closed in prayer we wanted answers, but all we felt was the weight of the questions. Our prayers were reverent but polite until one young woman began to pray. She was willing to "go there," breaking into the silence with wailing:

"We *need* you!"

"We *need* you!"

"We *need* you!"

In her voice I heard my cries on the lakeshore, Louis CK's roadside lament, the pleas of the psalmist and of all the generations who have cried out to God for salvation. This young woman who pastors an urban church, a church filled with overlooked people, knows how to say, "We *need* you!"

At that moment I understood why the church needs to hear from the poor and broken, the overlooked and marginalized. Not just because it's fair. Or because it's their turn. But because they model for us how to know our lack, how to feel our longing, how to cry out for help—all things we've forgotten. All the pieces were beginning to come together, and in this woman's honest vulnerability I felt a call to name our weakness and bring it to the world. I felt a call for the church to be willing to "go there," to feel our brokenness and longing for the sake of modeling it for each other.

Reflect

Who in the church is modeling for you this posture of crying out?

The final story, which felt like the last unraveling of the knot, is one I read in *The Guardian*. The article shares how as a younger man the author prided himself on his ability "to look at any ideology or any thought process and expose the inconsistencies." He saw the Bible as "the skinny 85-pound weakling for anyone looking to flex their scientific muscles" and loved to take down the arguments of Christians he met. Then he moved from his office job to work as an inner city photographer, capturing the lives of homeless drug addicts and prostitutes. What amazed him was how these people—who knew real brokenness—clung to God. He writes,

> In these last three years, out from behind my computers, I have been reminded that life is not rational and that everyone makes mistakes. Or, in biblical terms, we are all sinners. . . . On the streets the addicts, with their daily battles and proximity to death, have come to understand this viscerally. Many successful people don't. Their sense of entitlement and emotional distance has numbed their understanding of our fallibility. Soon I saw my

atheism for what it is: an intellectual belief most accessible to those who have done well.[5]

We may be tempted to respond with, "Yes, those nasty atheists, with their science and argumentative spirit. They should see their need for God." But I have to say that his description reminded me of what Christianity in our insulated culture can also be: an intellectual belief accessible to those who have done well.

> ### *Reflect*
>
> Who in the world needs to see your need for God and hear your crying out?

In Revelation 3, Jesus warns the believers at Laodicea that they're so lukewarm he's about to spew them from his mouth. When we read this passage, concerns that we may be lukewarm often make us resolve to be more outspoken about our faith. We ask ourselves, "When was the last time I posted a hard-nosed Christian standpoint online or argued about faith at work? Am I an activist for Christianity? How well could I defend everything I believe?"

But Jesus' entreaty to the Laodiceans is surprising. After calling them lukewarm, he challenges them: "You say, 'I am rich; I have acquired wealth and do not need a thing.' But you do not realize that you are wretched, pitiful, poor, blind and naked" (Revelation 3:17). Instead of calling us to move toward strength, Jesus calls us to move toward brokenness. "Lukewarm" is not "wussy." "Lukewarm" is resting on our own ability. "Lukewarm" is trying to be strong.

If we are honest, how much of our faith is in a set of doctrines? In a well-constructed argument? In technologies like ministry programs? In the latest book, the edgiest education? In easy access to food, running water, medicine, technology, safety? How do our security, wealth and intellectual strength mask our lack and our longing? How do they keep us from crying out to God?

In the Western world we're seeing Christian cultural institutions and traditions crumble. In response Christians are getting desperate. You don't have to look further than the latest online controversy where sarcastic Christians rage as they watch the disintegration of systems in which they've found centuries of security and identity. But the sarcasm and anger mask desperation and fear. I feel it too. Maybe because our hope is in our system: having our opinions voiced in the media, knowing people with our beliefs will fill roles of political power, trusting that store clerks will say "Merry Christmas" to us during the holidays.

But is this where our strength truly lies? Somehow the early church got along fine without cultural power. How has having economic and political power made us say, "I am rich; I have prospered and I need nothing"? The world does not need more anger, more argument, more human force. The world needs permission to acknowledge its humanity. Human beings, especially wealthy ones, need to know it's not shameful to be broken, desperate and inadequate, to sense a need beyond themselves.

My lakeshore lesson reminded me of my own vulnerability, and in Louis CK I saw that even outside the church other humans are waking

> The world I know, as a Christian, is the one in which we're a small minority.... I know there was another world before this one, in which Christianity was the unconsidered default state of the civilization, but it was dying when I was a child in the 1960s and 1970s, and it's gone now, and I don't think I would like it back. This way, Christianity is no one's vehicle for ambition. This way, Christianity has been detached from the self-importance of the self-important. . . . This way, the strangeness of Christianity can be visible again. Without the inevitability, without the static of privilege fuzzing the channel, we can pick out again more clearly the countercultural call it makes, to admit your lack of cool, and your incompleteness . . . and to find hope instead; a hope that counts upon, is kindly raised upon, the mess you actually are.
> **Francis Spufford**[6]

up to theirs. But we don't always know what to do with it. Tenebrae reminded me I'm part of an ancient tradition that used to know. And hearing the young urban pastor's prayers showed me there are still some in our midst who remember. The story of the softening of a skeptic as he watched broken people rely on God made me see how, more than our easy answers, it's our need for God that points others to him.

Reflect

How would your personal efforts and church efforts at justice, evangelism and outreach change if they were motivated by your own deep need? What solidarity could this reveal?

And so it's time to return to our great tradition of knowing our need. To remember it's blessed to be poor in spirit, to be mournful, meek, hungry for righteousness, merciful, pure in heart, peacemaking and persecuted. Our call is to see beyond the gloss and comfort of life in the developed world, to avoid the violence of a quick fix, to learn to listen for the sucking sound of that "forever empty." Our call is to admit how much we lack, how deeply we yearn. It may take losing our influence, our wealth, our connections, our institutions, our technology and everything else that gives us a sense of power for us to finally say, "We need you, God!" It will then be our task to wait and watch what becomes of the space we have left for him to fill. The sooner Christians can relearn this kind of lack and this kind of longing, the more we can remember our human hunger, the more help we'll be to this human world.[7]

Reflect

What situations in your life make you feel like you're sinking? When you're sinking, do you scramble to save yourself or know to cry out for help? Who needs to see your need for God?

Epilogue

Unfading Treasure
in Jars of Clay

nside each of us there's a tiny desert. And we work hard to keep it tidy. Or hidden. Or both. We armor our outer selves with anything hard and shiny enough to shield the hollowness. A being with an empty core needs to be careful.

But the ground in this internal desert is a thin crust. If we take time to visit this inner desert and do any digging, the shallow earth gives way around us and we find ourselves falling into an immense chasm. Fear fills our lungs and emerges as a wail into the expanses. Where will this falling take us? How is it possible we are even more empty than we knew? How can we fill it up? And quickly?

Our terrified screams turn to cries for God and we no longer know if we've landed or just become accustomed to falling. Before we can even name our need for him, the creator of the universe, who spoke light into being, speaks light into our hearts. We see for the first time the hugeness of the hollow within us and yet, when we see it by his light, there is no shame; he both reveals the emptiness and offers to complete it.

If we accept his offer, we find ourselves filled with his unfading, eternal treasure, a treasure that will take the rest of our lives to fathom. The freedom of the ever-increasing fullness of God now gives us courage to consider our outer shell. If we hold within us the Spirit of the living God, can we manage without our armor? We've worn it so long it's become part of us and it's painful to remove. When the final piece clanks to the ground we feel exposed yet weightless. Naked like a newborn, ready for life.

And so from our existence as an empty being in an impenetrable outer shell, we are given new life as filled beings in a crumbling husk. Our outer selves are overwhelmed and confused, inadequate and weak—one little stumble and we see the fragility of our clay selves. Entropy besets us: our minds are slow; our bodies are limited; our talents are underwhelming. All this is true. And yet it is only part of our truth. And it is only true for now.

There is a strange opportunity in the mismatch of our inner and outer selves. If we had perfect, powerful forms through which to express this treasure, we would seem to be expressing our own power. It's easy to long for a form that matches the fullness we now feel in our hearts. But this glory is housed in human bodies so that it will be obvious whose power is at work. To wish for more is to wish to be more than Jesus was.

So for now we live in this strange form and we don't lose heart, knowing that while outwardly we are wasting away, inwardly we are being renewed day by day. The Spirit of the risen Lord is ours. The world's entropy cannot touch our hearts. In unseen places something miraculous is happening: hidden among all the decay our spirits are getting younger, more courageous, more childlike. And this is not in spite of the challenges and brokenness but because of them. When we see weakness and failure as an invitation to rely on him, they become fuel for the inward renewal.

And so we set our eyes not on what is seen—our outer crumbling, our deep inadequacy—but on what is unseen. We fix our eyes on our true source of power and ask God to fix our eyes. As he does, our lives flow from that inner flourishing, even through a body that is dying, in a world that is fading. As we live with new eyes, we are astounded by the beauty of what we hold in our hearts, no less than the glory of God waiting to be expressed through human frailty.[1]

This is the most true thing I have ever known. And it's not only true for me; it's true for us all. I've watched how it's true for leaders who have to be honest about their own weakness and their need for God, how it's true for congregations as they watch their leaders' need for God and find in their own weakness their own need for God. It's true for those who have never known God as they watch his followers set aside performance and admit humanity. This kind of truth cannot be argued but reveals itself as we live it.

It's nothing less than the gospel, truly good news.

This honest, vulnerable approach shows itself true in Scripture, in our hearts, in our churches, in the world. It's invigorating to our personal faith, giving us hope, courage and freedom. It engages and gives grace to others, building leaders and churches. It resonates with the human heart, relates to the human condition, leaves room for human development. It is disarming and refreshing to those who don't know Christ. So what is keeping us from stepping into it? Only fear. But what have we to lose? What is a tiny, tidy desert compared to an eternal, unfading treasure?

Books should end with completion. Instead, it seems right to end with beginning. You may know less now than when you began but maybe that doesn't matter so much anymore. You may feel less competent in skills you once valued but maybe you have risky new skills that bring more joy. When you turn the last page of this book, you may be more aware than ever before of the clay jar you are. Now comes the joyful challenge, the bright burden, of living as one who houses a great treasure.

Discussion Guide

When you think of vulnerability in general, what comes to mind? When you think about your own vulnerability, how do you feel? What fears or concerns does it raise?

What is your main hesitation with vulnerability in your personal relationships? In your relationship with God? In your ministry?

How have you seen vulnerability done well? How have you seen it done poorly?

How have you seen God use someone else's willingness to be vulnerable?

How have you seen God use your willingness to be vulnerable?

In what ways could vulnerability benefit a ministry team? A Christian community? The way the world sees the church?

How would you like to move toward vulnerability in your personal faith?

How would you like to move toward vulnerability in your ministry?

What would it look like in your context to be the first to step toward vulnerability?

What does it mean to live as a clay jar that houses an unfading treasure?

How can your human frailty bring life to your inner renewal?

How will you share that?

Acknowledgments

The moments of recognizing strength in my weakness came from seeing it in the faces of others.

Thank you, Troy, Anthony, Nathan, Marty and Jo, for giving me the grace to practice in public and for being in this process with me.

Thank you, Jerry and all my huddle mates, for asking hard questions and being unafraid of the tears they brought.

Thank you, Kate, for being the kind of person who takes calls from hotel rooms.

Thank you, Jen and Shannon, for making a place where your pastor can be a person.

Thank you, J.R., for giving me a chance to tell this story the first time and for creating ways for me to keep shaping and telling it.

Thank you, Vikki, for being my guinea pig and showing me this hope was not only for me.

Thank you, Sandie, for helping me find the turning points among the tension.

Thank you, Dave, for naming (and living) this calling as an art.

Thank you, Al Hsu and all the folks at IVP, for thoughtfully shaping and sharing my story.

Thank you, Tom and Becky, for your faithful friendship.

Thank you, Steph and Dwight. You are our reward from a difficult time.

Thank you, Mum, Dad and Wendy, for a home that made it possible for me to believe I'm loved.

Thank you, Zoë and Kieran, for your comfort with childlikeness.

Thank you, Jamie, for giving me courage to find what you see in me.

Thank you, Jesus, for revealing, in your own broken self, the hope of a power beyond this world.

Notes

INTRODUCTION

[1]Henri J. M. Nouwen, *In the Name of Jesus: Reflections on Christian Leadership* (New York: Crossroad Publishing, 1989), p. 64.

[2]Dietrich Bonhoeffer, *Life Together* (San Francisco: Harper, 1954), p. 116.

[3]As far as I know. And I've looked. If you know of other lead pastors who are women in the US Christian Churches/Churches of Christ, please let me know!

[4]Eugene Peterson, *Eat This Book: A Conversation in the Art of Spiritual Reading* (Grand Rapids: Eerdmans, 2006), pp. 26-27.

[5]Esther Lightcap Meek, *A Little Manual for Knowing* (Eugene, OR: Cascade Books, 2014), p. 72.

1 FILLED WITH EMPTINESS

[1]Barbara Brown Taylor, *An Altar in the World: A Geography of Faith* (New York: Harper Collins, 2010), p. 78.

[2]Helen Keller, *The Open Door* (New York: Doubleday, 1957), p. 17.

[3]Brené Brown, "The Power of Vulnerability," TED, June 2010, www.ted.com /talks/brene_brown_on_vulnerability.

[4]Brennan Manning, *All Is Grace: A Ragamuffin Memoir* (Colorado Springs, CO: David C Cook, 2011), p. 17. Used by permission.

[5]Henri J. M. Nouwen, *In the Name of Jesus: Reflections on Christian Leadership* (New York: Crossroad Publishing, 1989), p. 30.

[6]I came across this invitation and challenge language in a 3DM discipleship training taught by Mike Breen.

[7]Esther Lightcap Meek, *A Little Manual for Knowing* (Eugene, OR: Cascade Books, 2014), pp. 35-36.

[8]When I've asked people to enter into this process, I've been interested to see how we are comfortable trusting God for help with a physical weakness, a way we feel inadequate or don't measure up, any kind of external limitation. But I've had many say to me, "What if my weakness is my own sin?" Why do we feel that's still our problem, that God won't help us until we're sinless? Instead, what would it look like if even our own sinfulness made us reach out for God instead of shy away in shame? See chapter 3 for more on this.

[9]Parts of this chapter are adapted from Mandy Smith, "Experts in Weakness," *Leaven Magazine* 22, no. 2 (2014), and Mandy Smith, "Experts in Weakness," *Leadership Journal*, April 2014, www.christianitytoday.com/le/2014/spring/experts-in-weakness.html.

2 WHAT MAKES US FEEL WEAK. AND WHAT DOESN'T

[1]Albert Borgmann, *Power Failure: Christianity in the Culture of Technology* (Grand Rapids: Brazos Press, 2003), pp. 29-31.

[2]This is a great question that gave me pause at the Epic Fail Pastors event, an event I highly recommend (see www.EpicFailEvents.com). Or read J. R. Briggs's book based on the event: *Fail: Finding Hope and Grace in the Midst of Ministry Failure* (Downers Grove, IL: InterVarsity Press, 2014).

3 SAVE ME!

[1]Brennan Manning, *The Ragamuffin Gospel* (Sisters, OR: Multnomah Publishers, 2000), pp. 18-20.

[2]If we're asking, "Well then, how much can I get away with and still get God's grace?" we're obviously asking the wrong question.

[3]Joe Simpson, *Touching the Void: The True Story of One Man's Miraculous Survival* (New York: HarperCollins, 1988). In case you're curious, he found a way out farther down and lived to tell the tale.

[4]James Choung has created a helpful way to describe the gospel. See his interview with Andy Crouch, "From Four Laws to Four Circles," *Christianity Today*, June 27, 2008, www.christianitytoday.com/ct/2008/july/11.31.html and his book *True Story: A Christianity Worth Believing In* (Downers Grove, IL: InterVarsity Press, 2008).

[5]Nathan Lutz, founder of TOAG Internships, in an email.

[6]Michael Frost and Alan Hirsch, *The Shaping of Things to Come: Innovation and Mission for the 21st Century* (Grand Rapids: Baker Books, 2013), p. 68.

[7]From my interview with Joe Boyd, "More Than a Performance," *Christianity*

Today, June 26, 2014, www.christianitytoday.com/parse/2014/june/bible -storyteller-joe-boyd.html.

[8]These approaches encourage Christians to share their own stories and develop relationships to earn the permission to share the gospel. See Michael L. Simpson's *Permission Evangelism: When to Talk, When to Walk* (Colorado Springs, CO: NexGen, 2003).

[9]Fil Anderson, *Breaking the Rules: Trading Performance for Intimacy with God* (Downers Grove, IL: InterVarsity Press, 2010), p. 81.

4 FEELING EXPOSED

[1]"Brené Brown on Empathy," an RSA Short animated by Katy Davis, http://brenebrown.com/2013/12/10/rsabear.

[2]"Fierce Tip of the Week: Pay Attention to Your Influence," *The Fierce Blog*, July 7, 2014, www.fierceinc.com/blog/fierce-conversations/fierce-tip-of-the -week-pay-attention-to-your-influence.

[3]For further reading, see Susan Scott, *Fierce Conversations: Achieving Success at Work and in Life One Conversation at a Time* (New York: Berkley Publishing, 2002), and Harriet Lerner, *The Dance of Connection: How to Talk to Someone When You're Mad, Hurt, Scared, Frustrated, Insulted, Betrayed, or Desperate* (New York: Harper, 2001).

[4]Dan Kindlon and Michael Thompson, *Raising Cain: Protecting the Emotional Life of Boys* (New York: Random House, 2000), pp. xiii, xix.

[5]*The Mask You Live In*, The Representation Project, www.therepresentation project.org/films/the-mask-you-live-in. For further reading, see Carolyn Custis James, *Malestrom: Manhood Swept into the Currents of a Changing World* (Grand Rapids: Zondervan, 2015) and *Half the Church: Recapturing God's Global Vision for Women* (Grand Rapids: Zondervan, 2011).

[6]Nancy R. Smith, "For Every Woman," Gender and Disaster Network, 1973, www.gdnonline.org/nancy-smith-poem.php.

[7]For further reading, see Daniel Goldman, *Emotional Intelligence: Why It Can Matter More Than IQ* (New York: Bantam, 2006).

[8]Peter Scazzero, *The Emotionally Healthy Church: A Strategy for Discipleship That Actually Changes Lives* (Grand Rapids: Zondervan, 2002), p. 20.

[9]Edwin H. Friedman, *A Failure of Nerve: Leadership in the Age of the Quick Fix* (New York: Seabury Books, 2007), p. 18.

[10]See more on rhythm in chapter 9.

[11]Sections of this chapter have appeared in Mandy Smith, "A Faithfulness

Deeper than Feeling," PARSE (blog), *Leadership Journal,* March 24, 2014, www.christianitytoday.com/parse/2014/march/faithfulness-deeper-than -feeling.html.

6 Letting the Bible Read Us

[1]Bob Hyatt, "Like Starving Chefs," PARSE (blog), *Leadership Journal,* July 21, 2014, www.christianitytoday.com/parse/2014/july/like-starving-chefs.html.

[2]Colin Brown, ed., *New International Dictionary of New Testament Theology* (Grand Rapids: Zondervan, 1986), 3:112. It may be interesting to see how words from the same root are used in Acts 22:2 and 1 Thessalonians 4:11.

[3]Esther Lightcap Meek, *A Little Manual for Knowing* (Eugene, OR: Cascade Books, 2014), pp. 95, 98.

[4]BibleGateway (www.biblegateway.com) has a variety of online audio Bibles, including one read by British actor David Suchet that has transformed my reflection on Scripture. If Johnny Cash is more your style, Audible (www .audible.com) has his reading.

[5]Examen.me (www.examen.me) is a helpful *lectio divina* tool.

7 Learning to Like the Mess

[1]Edwin H. Friedman, *A Failure of Nerve: Leadership in the Age of the Quick Fix* (New York: Seabury Books, 2007), p. 14.

[2]While we're not talking literally about buildings here, it's fascinating that Malcolm Gladwell in *The Tipping Point* talks about the number of genuine social connections human brains can handle (around 150) and how that shows itself in hunter-gatherer societies, military organizations, various religious traditions and some corporations, including Gore Associates (of Gore-Tex fame). The founder, Bill Gore, says that when his company builds a new plant, they build it with 150 parking spaces, and when the lot is full, it's time to build the next plant. See Malcolm Gladwell, *The Tipping Point: How Little Things Can Make A Big Difference* (New York: Back Bay, 2002), pp. 184-85.

[3]Human resources researchers are beginning to explore the concept of the human workplace, and their insights have implications for ministry. See Liz Ryan, "How to Build a Human Workplace," *Forbes,* January 23, 2015, www .forbes.com/sites/lizryan/2015/01/23/how-to-build-a-human-workplace. See also www.humanworkplace.com.

[4]Sam Wells, *Improvisation: The Drama of Christian Ethics* (Grand Rapids: Brazos Press, 2004), p. 69.

⁵A section of this chapter was published as Mandy Smith, "Play What You Feel: How Rediscovering Artistic Freedom Changed My Leadership," *Leadership Journal*, May 27, 2013, www.ctlibrary.com/le/2013/may-online -only/play-what-you-feel.html.

⁶Joan M. Erikson, *Wisdom and the Senses: The Way of Creativity* (New York: W. W. Norton, 1988), pp. 65, 67-68.

⁷Kathleen Norris, *The Cloister Walk* (New York: Riverhead Books, 1997), preface.

⁸Stuart Brown, *Play: How It Shapes the Brain, Opens the Imagination and Invigorates the Soul* (New York: Avery, 2009), p. 59.

⁹My previous book, *Making a Mess and Meeting God: Unruly Ideas and Everyday Experiments for Worship* (Cincinnati: Standard Publishing, 2010), includes some exercises to stretch our experimental and playful sides. Also check out Roger Von Oech, *A Kick in the Seat of the Pants: Using Your Explorer, Artist, Judge, and Warrior to Be More Creative* (New York: Perennial Library, 1986).

¹⁰Brennan Manning, *Ruthless Trust: The Ragamuffin's Path to God* (New York: HarperCollins, 2009), p. 5.

¹¹Adapted from Mandy Smith, "Confidence Without Clarity," *Leadership Journal*, November 2013, www.christianitytoday.com/le/2013/november-online -only/confidence-without-clarity.html.

¹²Brené Brown, *Daring Greatly: How the Courage to Be Vulnerable Transforms the Way We Live, Love, Parent and Lead* (New York: Gotham Books, 2012), pp. 174-75.

8 Changing the Mold

¹M. Rex Miller, *The Millennium Matrix: Reclaiming the Past, Reframing the Future of the Church* (San Francisco: Jossey Bass, 2004), pp. 154-55.

²Adam S. McHugh, *Introverts in the Church: Finding Our Place in an Extroverted Culture* (Downers Grove, IL: InterVarsity Press, 2009), p. 12.

³Alan Hirsch and Dave Ferguson, *On the Verge: A Journey into the Apostolic Future of the Church* (Grand Rapids: Zondervan, 2011), pp. 94-95.

⁴Stephen B. Sample, *The Contrarian's Guide to Leadership* (San Francisco: Jossey Bass, 2002).

⁵Sections of this chapter were published in Mandy Smith, "You Must Read This . . . Recognizing Leadership Potential," *ChristianStandard*, October 29, 2011, www.christianstandard.com/2011/10/you-must-read-this-recognizing -leadership-potential.

[6]See Ram Charan, Stephen Drotter and James Noel, *The Leadership Pipeline: How to Build the Leadership Powered Company* (San Francisco: Jossey Bass, 2011); Mike Breen, *Multiplying Missional Leaders* (Pawleys Island, SC: 3DM, 2012); Dave Ferguson and Jon Ferguson, *Exponential: How You and Your Friends Can Start a Missional Church Movement* (Grand Rapids: Zondervan, 2010).

9 TAKING OUR OWN SWEET TIME

[1]Brennan Manning quotes the motto of his friend Mary Michael O'Shaughnessy, "Today I will not should on myself," in *All Is Grace: A Ragamuffin Memoir* (Colorado Springs, CO: David C Cook, 2011), p. 187.

[2]J.R. Briggs, *Fail: Finding Hope and Grace in the Midst of Ministry Failure* (Downers Grove, IL: InterVarsity Press, 2014), pp. 46-47.

[3]"[By] attractional, we mean that the traditional church plants itself within a particular community, neighborhood or locale and expects that people will come to it to meet God and find fellowship with others. We don't claim that there's anything unbiblical about being attractive to unbelievers. . . . Nonetheless, when we say it is a flaw for the church to be attractional, we refer more to the missionary stance the church takes toward the broader host communities and cultures it inhabits. By anticipating that if they get their internal features right, people will flock to the services, the church betrays its belief in attractionalism." Michael Frost and Alan Hirsch, *The Shaping of Things to Come: Innovation and Mission for the Twenty-First Century Church* (Grand Rapids: Baker Books, 2013), p. 35.

[4]Carolyn Gregoire, "18 Things Highly Creative People Do Differently," *Huffington Post*, March 4, 2014, www.huffingtonpost.com/2014/03/04 /creativity-habits_n_4859769.html.

[5]Daniel J. Levitin, "Hit the Reset Button on Your Brain," *The New York Times*, August 9, 2014, www.nytimes.com/2014/08/10/opinion/sunday /hit-the-reset-button-in-your-brain.html.

[6]Tony Schwartz and Jim Loehr, *The Power of Full Engagement: Managing Energy, Not Time, Is the Key to High Performance and Personal Renewal* (New York: Free Press, 2003), p. 168.

[7]You may also be interested to read the weekly habits of five other pastors in Eric Mason et al., "How Does Your Week Look?," *Leadership Journal*, Winter 2015, www.christianitytoday.com/le/2015/winter/how-does-your-week-look .html.

[8]See 3D Movements at www.3dmovements.com.

[9]For further reading, see Alvin Rosenfeld and Nicole Wise, *The Over-Scheduled Child: Avoiding the Hyper-Parenting Trap* (New York: St. Martin's, 2000); Richard Florida, *The Rise of the Creative Class* (New York: Basic Books, 2011); and Daniel Pink, *A Whole New Mind* (New York: Berkley Publishing Group, 2005).

[10]Those driven by concerns that a human-scale life will mean their kids won't be a success will find comfort in William Fitzsimmons, Marlyn E. McGrath and Charles Ducey, "Time Out or Burn Out for the Next Generation," Harvard College Admission and Financial Aid, 2011, www.college.harvard .edu/admissions/preparing-college/should-i-take-time.

[11]Jeanne Sahadi, "Unlimited Vacation? It May Not Be as Cool as It Sounds," CNN Money, November 25, 2014, money.cnn.com/2014/11/19/pf/unlimited -vacation.

[12]Walter Brueggemann, *Sabbath as Resistance: Saying No to the Culture of Now* (Louisville, KY: Westminster John Knox, 2014), preface.

[13]Adapted from Mandy Smith, "Ritual: Lunch Break," *Geez Magazine*, May 24, 2012, www.geezmagazine.org/magazine/article/ritual-lunch-break.

10 THRIVING FOR OTHERS

[1]See John Drane, *The McDonaldization of the Church: Consumer Culture and the Church's Future* (Macon, GA: Smith and Helwys, 2001); J.R. Briggs, *Fail: Finding Hope and Grace in the Midst of Ministry Failure* (Downers Grove, IL: InterVarsity Press, 2014); and C. Christopher Smith and John Pattison, *Slow Church: Cultivating Community in the Patient Way of Jesus* (Downers Grove, IL: InterVarsity Press, 2014).

[2]"There's a Name for the Big Flaw in Our Obsession with Assessment and Metrics," *Pacific Standard*, November 13, 2014, www.psmag.com/navigation /books-and-culture/theres-name-big-flaw-obsession-assessment-metrics -93718.

[3]See Briggs, *Fail,* and Smith and Pattison, *Slow Church,* along with Paul Sparks, Tim Soerens and Dwight Friesen, *The New Parish: How Neighborhood Churches Are Transforming Mission, Discipleship and Community* (Downers Grove, IL: InterVarsity Press, 2014).

[4]Arianna Huffington, *Thrive: The Third Metric of Redefining Success* (New York: Harmony Books, 2014), p. 2.

[5]Eugene Peterson, *Working the Angles: The Shape of Personal Integrity* (Grand Rapids: Eerdmans, 2000), p. 2.

[6]Exploring Christian hospitality was incredibly helpful in this process, especially Christine Pohl's *Making Room: Recovering Hospitality as a Christian Tradition* (Grand Rapids: Eerdmans, 1999).

[7]A version of this section was published as Mandy Smith, "Is It Selfish to Say No?," *Leadership Journal*, February 2015, www.christianitytoday.com/le/2015 /february-online-only/is-it-selfish-to-say-no.html.

[8]Anne Rice, *Christ the Lord: The Road to Cana* (New York: Alfred A. Knopf, 2008), pp. 32-33.

[9]Michael Soussan and Elizabeth Weingarten, "What Really Scares Terrorists," CNN, December 26, 2014, www.cnn.com/2014/12/26/opinion/soussan -weingarten-gender-equality.

[10]"The industrialization of the church has, significantly, paralleled the industrialization of agriculture and the near demise of the family farm. . . . Western Christianity has similarly adopted shortcuts that are the church equivalent of imposing a mechanistic mindset onto a biological world." Smith and Pattison, *Slow Church*, p. 14.

[11]However, it is interesting that the writers of the New Testament weren't entirely uninterested in the size of crowds or number of conversions.

11 WELCOME TO THE PROCESS

[1]Esther Lightcap Meek, "When Loving Is Knowing," PARSE (blog), *Leadership Journal*, September 2104, christianitytoday.com/parse/2014/september /when-loving-is-knowing.html.

[2]Thank you to Christine Pohl for her "living into a new creation" language from the Slow Church Conference, Englewood Christian Church, April 2014.

[3]For further reading, see John Howard Yoder, *Body Politics: Five Practices of the Christian Community Before the Watching World* (Scottsdale, PA: Herald Press, 2001); C. Christopher Smith and John Pattison, *Slow Church: Cultivating Community in the Patient Way of Jesus* (Downers Grove, IL: InterVarsity Press, 2014); Ronald Grimes, *Ritual Criticism* (Columbia, SC: University of South Carolina Press, 1990); and Dietrich Bonhoeffer, *Life Together* (San Francisco: Harper, 1954).

[4]Lauren Winner, *Mudhouse Sabbath: An Invitation to a Life of Spiritual Discipline* (Brewster, MA: Paraclete Press, 2007), p. ix.

[5]Ronald Grimes, *Ritual Criticism* (Columbia, SC: University of South Carolina Press, 1990), p. 148.

[6]Henri J. M. Nouwen, *In the Name of Jesus: Reflections on Christian Leadership*

(New York: Crossroad Publishing, 1989), p. 69.

[7]Curt Thompson, *Anatomy of the Soul: Surprising Connections Between Neuroscience and Spiritual Practices That Can Transform Your Life and Relationships* (Carol Stream, IL: Tyndale House, 2010), p. 102.

12 THE RIGHT KIND OF DESPERATE

[1]Mark Van Steenwyk, *The Unkingdom of God: Embracing the Subversive Power of Repentance* (Downers Grove, IL: InterVarsity Press, 2013), p. 43.

[2]John Gravois, "A Toast Story," *Pacific Standard,* January 13, 2014, www.psmag .com/navigation/health-and-behavior/toast-story-latest-artisanal-food -craze-72676.

[3]"Louis CK Hates Cell Phones," TeamCoco, September 2013, www.teamcoco .com/video/louis-ck-springsteen-cell-phone.

[4]From the order of service for the St. Peter in Chains, Cincinnati, Tenebrae service; adapted from Psalm 69.

[5]Chris Arnade, "The People Who Challenged My Atheism Most Were Drug Addicts and Prostitutes," *The Guardian,* December 24, 2013, www.theguardian .com/commentisfree/2013/dec/24/atheism-richard-dawkins-challenge -beliefs-homeless.

[6]Francis Spufford, *Unapologetic: Why, Despite Everything, Christianity Can Still Make Surprising Emotional Sense* (New York: HarperOne, 2012), pp. 218-19.

[7]Sections of this chapter appeared as Mandy Smith, "The Right Kind of Desperate," PARSE (blog), *Leadership Journal,* February 10, 2014, www .christianitytoday.com/parse/2014/february/right-kind-of-desperate.html.

EPILOGUE

[1]This is 2 Corinthians 4 in my own words.

About the Author

Originally from Australia, Mandy is lead pastor of University Christian Church, a Cincinnati campus and neighborhood congregation with its own fair-trade café (see universitychristianchurch .net and rohsstreetcafe.com). She is the author of *Making a Mess and Meeting God: Unruly Ideas and Everyday Experiments for Worship*, creator of The Collect, a citywide trash-to-art project, and a regular contributor to *Christianity Today*'s PARSE site. Mandy is married to Dr. Jamie Smith, New Testament professor at Cincinnati Christian University, and they live with their two children in a little house where the teapot is always warm.